RAND

Three Strikes and You're Out

Estimated Benefits and Costs of California's New Mandatory-Sentencing Law

Peter W. Greenwood, C. Peter Rydell,
Allan F. Abrahamse, Jonathan P. Caulkins,
James Chiesa, Karyn E. Model, Stephen P. Klein

The research described in this report was supported by RAND using its own research funds.

ISBN: 0-8330-1597-4

Published 1994 by RAND

1700 Main Street, P.O. Box 2138, Santa Monica, CA 90407-2138

To order RAND documents or to obtain additional information, contact Distribution Services: Telephone: (310) 451-7002; Fax: (310) 451-6915; Internet: order@rand.org.

Preface

This report documents an analysis of the benefits and costs of California's new "three-strikes" law mandating lengthier sentences for repeat offenders, along with various alternatives to that law. Benefits are expressed in terms of crime reduction, and estimated costs consist of the dollars spent by the various components of the criminal justice system.

This analysis has three objectives. The first is to inform the public debate over Proposition 184 on the November 1994 California statewide ballot. That proposition puts the content of the recently passed three-strikes law to a vote of the people. Second, if the proposition is rejected, legislators may consider replacing the current law with a different version. Thus, we have analyzed alternatives to the current law that accomplish some of the same purposes but with different benefits and costs. Third, many other states are considering three-strikes laws. Although these often differ in important respects from the California law, the methods and results developed here may prove informative to the debates over such laws.

This project was funded by RAND as part of its mission to bring analysis to bear on important public policy issues.

Contents

Figures

Tables

Summary

Public outrage over crime has found political expression in the proposal and enactment of various laws mandating lengthy sentences for repeat felons. Put forward under the slogan "three strikes and you're out," these laws generally prescribe that felons found guilty of a third serious crime be locked up for 25 years to life. The California law, which went into effect in March 1994, may be the most sweeping of these. Although the first two "strikes" accrue for serious felonies, the crime that triggers the life sentence can be *any* felony. Furthermore, the law doubles sentences for a second strike, requires that these extended sentences be served in prison (rather than in jail or on probation), and limits "good time" earned during prison to 20 percent of the sentence given (rather than 50 percent, as under the previous law).

In November, Californians will vote on the initiative proposition that gave the legislature its impetus to pass the new law. The text of the initiative and the text of the law are essentially the same. Should Californians approve the initiative and so ratify the legislature's action? Or should they reject it, sending the message that legislators should reconsider the new law, perhaps in favor of one of the competing three-strikes alternatives? What about other states? Should they follow California's lead?

In reaching a decision, Californians will naturally be affected by a variety of subjective factors, for example, fear of crime, sympathy for victims and their families, and anger at violent criminals. But voters should also have access to hard evidence regarding the implications of the law: How much crime reduction can they expect from the three-strikes law? And how much will it cost? What about the alternatives? And where will the money come from?

We undertook to answer these questions. We constructed and ran analytic models predicting how populations of offenders on the street and in prison would change under the new law and under various alternatives, including the previous law. Using data on these populations, we estimated crime rates and costs. Here is what we found.

What Will Be the Benefits and Costs of the New Law?

If fully implemented as written, the new law will reduce serious felonies committed by adults[1] in California between 22 and 34 percent below what would have occurred had the previous law remained in effect. About a third of the felonies eliminated will be violent crimes such as murder, rape, and assaults causing great bodily injury. The other two-thirds will be less violent but still serious felonies, including less injurious assaults, most robberies, and burglaries of residences.

This reduction in crime will be bought at a cost of an extra $4.5 billion to $6.5 billion per year in current dollars, compared to what would have been spent had the previous law remained in effect. The intent of the three-strikes law is, of course, to lock up repeat offenders longer, and that requires the construction and operation of more prisons. Some police and court costs may be saved in not having to deal so often with such offenders once they are locked up, but greater prison costs overwhelm such savings.

What About the Alternatives?

The new three-strikes law has been criticized by some for casting too wide a net. It is argued that the public is not really as concerned about minor felonies or even residential burglaries as it is about truly violent crimes and that it will not want to pay to keep less violent felons locked up. Indeed, our analysis showed that, more often than not, the third strike will accrue for a minor felony such as motor vehicle theft, as opposed to one of the serious crimes mentioned above.

In view of the width of the "net" and the power of the less-publicized provisions of the new law, could an alternative be constructed in which some benefit would be sacrificed to achieve great savings? What if there were no third-strike provision? Or, what if the extended sentences applied only if a violent felony were committed? What about one of the alternatives considered by the legislature, the "Rainey bill," which would have been harsher on violent felons and more lenient on others? Finally, what would happen if the state got rid of "strikes" and instead guaranteed that those convicted of a serious crime serve their full sentence? In other words, what about adopting a law that sends all those convicted of a serious felony to prison, eliminates "good time" for such felons, and shifts some minor felons from prison to probation?

---

[1]Juvenile offenders will not be affected by this law. They now account for about one-sixth of all arrests for violent crimes.

Figures S.1 and S.2 compare the benefits and costs of the new law and these alternatives, relative to the old law. As you might expect, for the most part, the more focused alternatives would be both less costly than the new law and less effective at reducing crime.[2] Some of them would not be *that much* less effective, though. For example, the second-strike-only alternative would be 85 percent as effective as the new law. This has an interesting implication: Only 15 percent of the new law's crime reduction effect will come from its most publicized provision—the third strike.

But for all the alternatives to the new law, the cost would drop more than the effectiveness. For example, applying the new law's penalties only to violent felons would save half its extra cost but retain two-thirds of its effectiveness.

Cost-effectiveness, though, is not necessarily the most important criterion. To some people, a reduction in serious crime on the order of 30 percent would be attractive no matter what the cost. However, it seems unlikely that anyone would want to pay more for that than they had to. In this context, the guaranteed-full-term alternative could be of interest, for it would be just as effective as the new law at substantially lower cost. The advantages of this alternative point up the shortcomings of the new law: The full-term alternative would increase sentences for all serious offenders—even first-timers who are

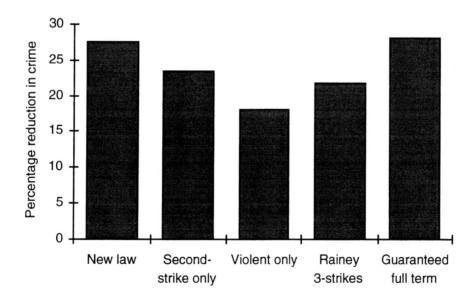

Figure S.1—Percentage Reduction in Serious Crime from New Law and Alternatives

---

[2]For these figures, we take the estimated benefits and costs of the new law from the middle of the ranges given above—28 percent and $5.5 billion.

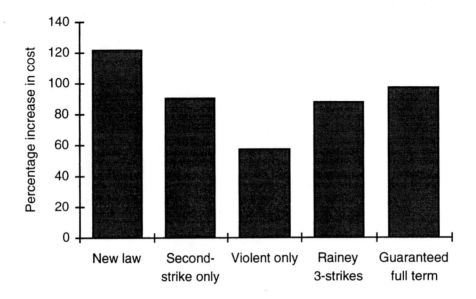

Figure S.2—Percentage Increase in Cost from New Law and Alternatives

near the beginning of their criminal careers—and pay for it by not imprisoning many minor felons. The new law, in contrast, ignores first-time serious offenders and instead expends large amounts of money keeping older criminals— including many convicted of minor offenses—locked up well past the time when they might have given up on crime anyway.

Where Will the Money Come From?

The money to finance three strikes will have to come from somewhere. The choices, however, are limited. Figure S.3 shows the current allocation of expenditures from the state's general fund. Proposition 98 locked into the state constitution a minimum level of spending on K–12 education that is expected to increase dramatically in the coming years—from 36 percent of the general fund now to 47 percent in 2002. Health and welfare costs have been going up for a long time and show no signs of leveling off. The new three-strikes law will double the fraction of the general fund consumed by the Department of Corrections. Clearly, these increases will put enormous pressure on everything else the state spends money on (see Figure S.4). That includes, most prominently, college education, but also a variety of other services ranging from controlling environmental pollution through managing parks and fighting brush fires to regulating insurance and other industries.

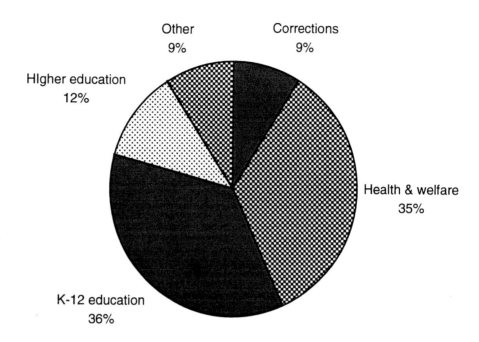

Figure S.3—Distribution of California General-Fund Appropriations, FY94

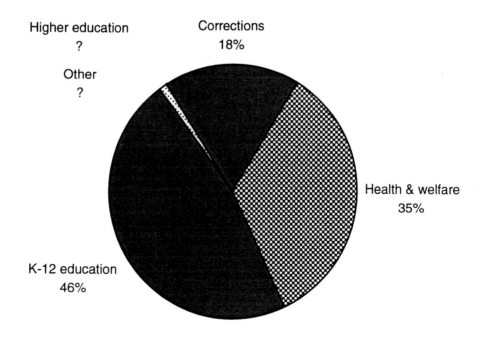

Assumes no increase in health & welfare (unlikely).

Figure S.4—Budgetary Squeeze on Higher Education and Other Services, FY02

It seems unlikely that Californians will put up with drastic reductions in these services, but increased taxes are decidedly unpopular. Clearly, something's got to give. It may be the three-strikes law itself. Criminal justice officials may simply not have the money to fully implement it. If that turns out to be the case, the new law will have less effect on serious crime than that estimated here. How much less is impossible to predict.

Acknowledgments

We thank Albert P. Williams, RAND Corporate Research Manager, Social Policy, for encouraging and supporting this study. We also thank the numerous agencies of California's state government that helped us to assemble the information used in the model. We particularly appreciate the assistance we received from the Department of Corrections, the Department of Justice, and the Legislative Analyst's Office. (This assistance took the form of information provided; it should not be inferred that these agencies endorse our findings.)

Susan Turner at RAND provided invaluable guidance in locating and interpreting key criminal justice statistics, and Stephen J. Carroll provided information on state fiscal trends. Tom Lucas and Mark Peterson provided thoughtful reviews, and Daniel A. Relles also contributed suggestions and coordinated the review process.

1. Introduction

Over the last year, public outrage over crime has found political expression in the proposal and enactment of various laws mandating very long sentences for repeat felons. Laws of this type, often termed "three strikes and you're out," have been passed by overwhelming margins in the states of Washington and California, and more than 30 other states have similar statutes under active consideration (Rohter, 1994).

Although all the proposed statutes would increase sentences substantially, they differ in the number and types of offenders they would affect. The new federal crime law, for example, would affect only the small number of defendants in federal courts who have accumulated three convictions for crimes involving serious injuries to their victims. Others would affect a large percentage of all defendants. The California law mandates 25 years to life in prison for an offender convicted of any felony following two prior convictions for serious crimes. It also doubles sentences on the second "strike," requires consecutive sentences for multiple counts, and limits "good time" credits. (For the text of the law, see Appendix A.)

The basic arguments advanced by proponents of the three-strikes concept are that

- It will protect the public by incapacitating (removing from society) those chronic offenders who have demonstrated by their acts that they are both dangerous and unwilling to reform.

- It will deter repeat offenders still on the street from committing further felonies.

- It will save money by cutting down on the number of times that career criminals need to be processed by the system.

- It is the "right thing to do." Aside from the savings and other effects, justice demands that those who repeatedly cause injury and loss to others have their freedom revoked.

Critics of the concept argue that

- Substantial increases in the use of imprisonment over the past decade have had little, if any, effect on violent-crime rates.

- Life terms for three-time losers will require the allotment of expensive prison space to offenders who are well past their peak ages of criminal activity.

- The demand for jury trials, caused by the law's restrictions on plea bargaining, will actually raise the costs of the criminal justice system and cause further delays in resolving criminal cases.

- The same amount of money applied to measures other than three strikes would reduce crime by a greater amount.

- The third-strike penalty is an unduly harsh one for criminals convicted of certain felonies such as drug possession.

Thus, although some of the debate is cast in moral terms, most of the disagreements are over questions that lend themselves to quantitative analysis. Little such analysis has appeared. To the average citizen, of course, increased punishment for serious crimes has intuitive appeal. But, as decisions approach in California and other states, voters may want to know just how much crime reduction they are getting for their money. Could they do as well for less money? And just what is the total cost of the law? Citizens are not getting much information on that from the law itself, the media, or their elected representatives. The law bears no explicit price tag; the media are better at depicting crime's human tragedy than at drawing up balance sheets; and politicians have at last found a cause that will offend no powerful interest group.

The analysis described in this report is designed to help clarify the ongoing debate over this issue by providing unbiased estimates of the likely effects of the proposed laws. These estimates are based on a mathematical model that tracks the flow of criminals through the justice system, calculates the costs of running the system, and predicts the number of crimes criminals commit when on the street. The model permits us to explore the extent to which these estimates change with changes in critical assumptions regarding the behavior of offenders and the response of the criminal justice system to the various provisions of the law.

It is our hope that this analysis will inform voter reaction in California to Proposition 184 on the November 1994 ballot, which is almost identical to the law passed by the legislature earlier this year.[1] Our analysis includes different versions of the three-strikes law, including an alternative considered by the legislature. Although these are not on the ballot, the legislature may review

---

[1] Passage of the initiative would have the practical effect of making the three-strikes law harder to repeal or to amend in ways that do not further its purpose, as such actions could be taken only by initiative.

them as possible substitutes for the current law should voters reject the three-strikes ballot initiative. We also hope our analysis will enlighten the ongoing debate over three-strikes proposals in other states.

We begin with a detailed summary of the alternative measures we consider (Section 2). We then describe how we modeled crime and imprisonment (Section 3) and present the results of our analysis (Section 4). The findings include reductions in crime and increases in costs projected for the previous law, the new law, and the various alternatives, along with anticipated trends in benefits and costs. Finally, we place the costs in budgetary perspective (Section 5).

2. Sentencing Alternatives for Repeat Offenders

California, along with the rest of the nation, experienced a general rise in reported crime rates in the 1970s and 1980s, but both the reported rates and victimization surveys show crime rates steady or declining over the past 15 years. Reported crime rates peaked around 1980 and declined steadily through 1985 when they again began to advance, though very slowly (see Figure 2.1).[1]

Violent crime (murders, rapes, and some robberies and assaults), on the other hand, rose more swiftly after the early 1980s decline (see Figure 2.2). Though still only one-sixth of the total crime rate, violent crime has doubled over the last 20 years.

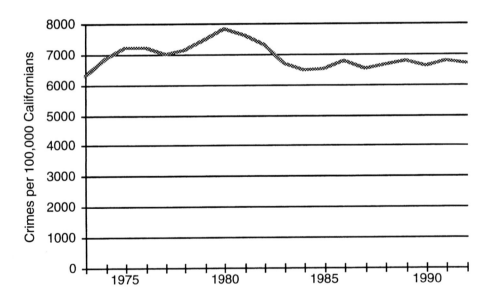

Figure 2.1—California Crime Rate, 1973–1992

---

[1]California Department of Justice (1992a).

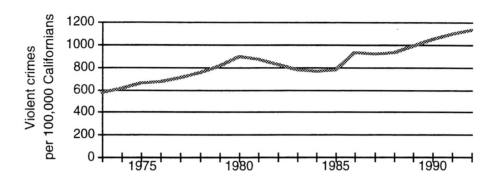

Figure 2.2—California Violent-Crime Rate, 1973–1992

Like many states, California began toughening its sentencing policies and adding prison capacity in the early 1980s, just as crime rates began a modest five-year decline. In fact, California was the leader among states in this trend, tripling its prison population in the decade since 1982. Between 1984 and 1991, more than 1000 bills were passed by the California legislature to change felony and misdemeanor statutes. Virtually none of these bills decreased sentences. Many lengthened them. This trend culminated in the introduction of several bills in this past legislative session, all of which required imprisonment of repeat felons for 25 years to life.

However, although the alternative measures' overall thrust was similar, they varied significantly in the offenders they targeted and in some of the sanctions they imposed. We evaluate two of those proposed laws (including the new three-strikes law) and three other alternative policies for increasing sentences of repeat offenders. We compare each of those to the previous law. To understand the differences among the various alternatives, one must understand what is meant by "serious" and "violent" felonies in California.[2]

The exact definition of serious and violent requires detailed lists of penal code violations (given in Appendix B). Generally speaking, violent crimes involve injuries to victims or, in some cases, threat with a deadly weapon. Serious crimes include virtually all violent crimes,[3] plus others where there is a potential for injury to victims. To understand the distinction between serious and violent, it may be helpful to compare these California categories with the FBI Uniform Crime Reports (UCR) index categories. Crimes that are *serious but not violent*

---

[2]We emphasize that, although we talk about "crime" and "crime rates," the three-strikes law and the analysis of alternatives in this report deal with *felonies* alone—and with *adult* felonies alone.

[3]Because of this, *when we say "serious crime" in this report, we include violent crime,* unless we specify otherwise.

include almost all arsons, and about half of robberies, assaults, and burglaries. *Violent crimes* include all murders, most rapes, and about half of robberies and assaults.[4] (Details of this comparison are presented in Appendix B, with an explanation of the breakdown between serious and violent for each FBI crime category.)

In addition to "violent" and "serious but not violent," we also define in our analysis a "minor" category that consists of all felonies that are not serious. These include such FBI index crimes as thefts and nonresidential burglaries, along with crimes not on the index, such as forgery, fraud, and drug offenses. With these definitions in mind, let us now identify the provisions of the alternatives we evaluate. (The provisions are summarized in Table 2.1. Key provisions serving as inputs to our quantitative analysis are presented comparatively in Appendix C.)

Previous Law

California is a determinate-sentencing state: Judges have few choices in sentencing. Instead, the legislature specifies prison terms for particular categories of crime, as well as additions to those sentences for specified circumstances, e.g., prior record. There were several repeat-offender provisions in effect before passage of the new three-strikes law. For example, a person convicted of a serious felony could be sentenced to five additional years in prison for each previous serious-felony conviction. Other prior laws included third- and fourth-strike provisions triggered by the infliction of great bodily injury or use of force likely to produce such injury. Those convicted of such crimes after having two prior prison terms for violent felonies could get 20 years to life. Those with three prior prison terms could get life without parole. However, previous law also reduced the length of prison sentences by allowing credit for work time and good behavior up to 50 percent of the sentence. It also permitted probation as a sentence for a person convicted of a felony unless probation was specifically proscribed for that crime.

In actual practice, the tough repeat-offender provisions have been partially vitiated by the lenient "good time" credits and by plea bargaining. Even after the increase in sentence severity of recent years, many felony convictions—even violent-felony convictions—do not result in a prison term. In our analysis, we

---

[4]The definitions of "serious" and "violent" follow California law and should not be read as reflecting the authors' judgment as to what crimes should be regarded as "serious" or "violent" as the terms are used in common parlance. For example, assaults might seem to be inherently violent, but not all assaults are classified as "violent" under California law.

Table 2.1

Alternatives Evaluated

Alternative	Second-Strike Sentence	Third-Strike Sentence	Is Prison Required?	"Good Time" Allowed
Previous law	Extra 5 yr[a]	Extra 10 yr for 3rd serious conviction; 20 yr to life for 3rd violent-felony incarceration	No	Up to 50 percent of sentence
Jones 3-strikes	Double the nominal sentence[b]	25 yr to life	Yes, if sentence is enhanced	Limited to 20 percent after 1st strike
Jones 2nd strike only	Double the nominal sentence	Double the nominal sentence	Yes, if sentence is enhanced	Limited to 20 percent after 1st strike
Jones violent only	Double the nominal sentence if violent	25 yr to life if violent	Yes, for violent 2nd or 3rd strike	Limited to 20 percent for violent 2nd or 3rd strike
Rainey 3-strikes	Extra 10 yr for 2nd violent-felony incarceration	25 yr to life	Yes, for serious on 2nd or 3rd strike	None if violent, or 3rd strike
Guaranteed full term	Same as previous law	Same as previous law	Yes, if serious[c]	None if serious

NOTES: "Serious" incorporates violent.

For all alternatives, a strike accrues on conviction of a serious felony; for Jones three-strikes, the third strike accrues on conviction of any felony. A nominal sentence is that provided by law for the crime for which the offender is convicted (no enhancements); treated as actual average sentence under previous law in quantitative analysis. For excluded cases, present law applies (e.g., if table text says, "for violent 2nd or 3rd strike," present law applies for serious nonviolent).

[a]Sentences for previous law are as given by statute. In quantitative analysis, sentences input are actual averages (used as baseline for other alternatives), and Jones three-strikes criteria are adopted (to permit use of actual-average baseline; also explained in Appendix C; applies also to Rainey and full-term alternative).

[b]Also applies to minor felony following one strike (though no second strike accrues in this case).

[c]This alternative also provides that half of all minor felons are not sentenced to prison.

used both the sentencing rules and the average actual sentences to estimate time served for violent, serious but not violent, and minor crimes.

Jones Three-Strikes

We refer to the three-strikes bill (AB 971) signed into law by Governor Wilson in March 1994 as the Jones law, after one of the legislation's sponsors. First and second strikes are convictions for serious felonies (whether violent or not). The third strike is a conviction for any felony. All persons receiving a second or third strike go to prison.

Since good-time credits of 20 percent are still allowed, we assume for our analysis that the average time served is 80 percent of the nominal sentence. For conviction of any felony with one prior strike, the nominal sentence is double the nominal sentence under the previous law, plus the previous law's enhancements. So, to calculate the total actual prison sentence for a second strike, we used 80 percent of double the average nominal sentence (specific to the nature of the crime) under the previous law. Persons convicted of any felony with two prior strikes receive a nominal sentence of at least 25 years to life. The 20 percent good-time provision makes the actual sentence at least 20 years to life. In our analysis, we treat this as 20 years in prison.[5]

It is worth noting that neither the Jones three-strikes law nor any of the alternatives changes sentencing policies for juveniles, who are responsible for at least one-sixth of serious crime in California.

Jones Second-Strike Only

As the name "three strikes" emphasizes, public discussion of the Jones three-strikes law focuses on the third strike. However, as just noted, the law provides for a doubling of nominal sentences for second-strike offenders—and mandates prison time for all such offenders. How much of the effect of the Jones law will come from the second-strike provisions? Or, to put it another way, what does the third-strike provision add? To find out, we constructed an alternative law with the same provisions as the Jones law except that conviction of any felony with one or more prior strikes results in a doubling of the nominal sentence for the latest crime (in other words, no automatic 20-year term for a third strike).

Jones Violent Only

The crimes that have driven the three-strikes movement are largely violent (e.g., the Klaas and Reynolds murders). Violent crimes, however, occur much less frequently than do such crimes as residential burglary and unarmed robbery, which, though serious, are not violent. Does the Jones law cast too wide a net in imposing repeat-offender penalties on persons convicted of crimes that are serious but not violent? We created an alternative formulation of the Jones law that allows serious, nonviolent crimes to count as strikes, but does not invoke the Jones law's penalties unless a conviction is for a violent crime. For example, an

---

[5]This should conservatively bias estimates of crime reduction and costs (and should, as will become clearer in Section 4, result in generous estimates of cost-effectiveness). Other approximations and assumptions have opposite effects (see Section 3).

offender with two serious, nonviolent convictions and a violent third conviction would get 25 years to life. An offender with the same prior convictions and a serious, nonviolent third conviction would receive the same sentence as he would have under the previous law (including 50 percent "good-time" credit).

Rainey Three-Strikes

Among the three-strikes bills considered by the legislature was AB 1568, known as the Rainey bill after its author. The Rainey bill maintained the previous law's five-year-per-strike sanctions for serious, nonviolent convictions, but raises the violent-conviction sanction to ten years per previous incarceration. Like the Jones law, Rainey imposed a third-strike penalty of 25 years to life, but it required that the third strike be a serious felony and allowed no good time at all for violent felons on any strike.

Guaranteed Full Term

For the final alternative, we made a significant departure from the three-strikes variants in an attempt to come up with an option that would reduce serious crime as much as possible at less cost. We believed we might achieve this goal with an alternative containing only three provisions. First, all convictions for serious or violent felonies (even those with no prior strikes) result in a prison term. Second, no good time is allowed for people sent to prison for serious crimes. Third, to reduce costs while minimizing the effect on crime, we cut in half the proportion of people convicted of minor crimes who receive prison terms (proportionately increasing the fractions who are sent to jail only—as opposed to prison—or who are not incarcerated at all). For convenience, we refer to this as the "guaranteed-full-term" alternative but note that that applies only to convictions for serious felonies.

3. How the Analysis Was Done

In this section, we review the approach we took in conducting our analysis. We begin with a general overview of the way we modeled offender populations. We then describe how we simulated the different aspects of offenders and offenses. We conclude with a presentation of the factors underlying our cost estimates and some key limitations in our analytic approach.

Projecting Offender Populations

Our analysis has two principal policy-relevant outputs—crime and criminal justice system costs. We want to know how much the felony crime rate is reduced by keeping repeat offenders locked up, and we want to know how much it costs to keep them locked up. The crime rate depends on the number of offenders on the street, and the added cost depends principally on the number of offenders incarcerated. Thus, we have constructed a mathematical model (diagrammed schematically in Figure 3.1) that predicts the number of offenders on the street and in prison. The number of offenders on the street depends on four factors:

- The rate at which people who have not yet committed a felony begin a criminal career.

- The rate at which offenders desist from crime.

- The rate at which offenders are removed from the street through incarceration.

- The rate at which incarcerated offenders are released.

The prison population is usefully divided into those who would commit felonies again if released from prison and those who would not.[1] This is an important distinction because, if the objective is to keep felons locked up to ensure they do not commit more crimes, keeping ex-felons locked up costs money with no gain.[2] As sentences wear on, some offenders may reach a point at which they

---

[1]We define an ex-offender pool because it allows us to compute the number of crimes averted by incapacitation. This in no way presupposes the ability to determine which *individuals* have desisted.

[2]Of course, there are other reasons to keep ex-felons locked up. A long sentence might deter others from committing similar crimes (although the evidence for this is weak). Also, many people

Nonoffenders   Offenders

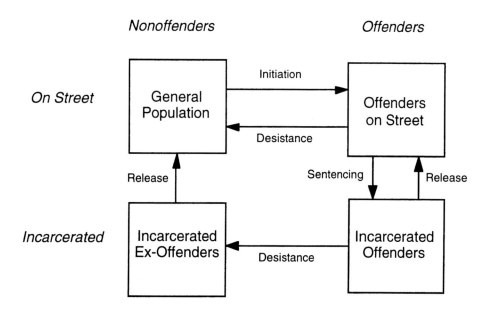

Figure 3.1—Criminal Dynamics

give up on a life of crime. Thus, the number of dangerous criminals in prison depends on three rates: the rate at which offenders on the street are incarcerated, the rate at which still-dangerous criminals are released from prison, and the rate at which incarcerated felons stop being dangerous.

Of the rates (arrows) shown in Figure 3.1, the two release rates are derived from sentence lengths associated with the various policies described in Section 2. Sentencing rates are derived from data on arrests per crime and convictions per arrest and, again, from the sentencing provisions in whichever alternative law is under consideration. We infer annual desistance rates from what is known about the length of criminal careers (they are on the order of 10 years long on average; see Blumstein et al., 1986). We assume that initiation into the criminal population is proportional to the state's population.[3] (These rates are examined in detail in Appendixes D and E.)

Projecting Offense Rates

As mentioned above, we use the number of offenders on the street to derive the crime rate, and we use the number of incarcerated offenders (among other

---

feel that a crime warrants a punishment of a certain length regardless of whether the criminal's state of mind changes during that period.

[3]We use U.S. Bureau of the Census estimates for current and projected state populations.

things) to derive costs. How is the crime rate related to the number of offenders on the street?

A common way to mathematically model criminals' offending patterns was pioneered by Shinnar and Shinnar (1975). The rates at which active criminals commit crimes, at which crimes lead to arrests, and at which criminals desist or "retire" are assumed to be represented by independent Poisson processes. A Poisson process is one in which the *average* frequency of occurrence of events (e.g., crimes) is constant, but events occur at random intervals. In fact, Poisson processes are completely random in the sense that knowing how long it has been since the last event does not help in predicting how long it will be until the next one. Thus, active offenders commit crimes at a constant average rate, but any two consecutive crimes might be a day apart or a month apart. Also, the probability that any given offense will lead to an arrest is constant. The *independence* of the Poisson processes refers to the lack of influence of one upon the other. For example, the probability that an active offender will desist at any given time is unrelated to how many crimes he or she has committed.

This simple model, like all models, ignores much of the complexity of real-world offending patterns. For example, offenders go on crime sprees; it is unlikely that a crime would be committed (or an offender rearrested) shortly following an arrest, when the offender would still be in custody; and it is more likely that a very old offender will desist from crime in the next month than that a young one will. Despite such imprecisions, the Poisson-based model has proven useful in modeling criminal behavior at the aggregate level.

Differences in Offense Rates

Not all criminals are equally active. Indeed, both arrest records and self-report surveys suggest that there are enormous differences in individual offense rates. These differences can be modeled by defining different values for rates of offense, arrest, and desistance, i.e., by defining different classes of criminals. Pragmatically, keeping track of many different classes of criminals is cumbersome. More important, there are precious few data available for estimating the rates (see Appendix D), and the more classes, the more parameters one must estimate.

Hence we model just two classes of offenders. We divide the population of incarcerated offenders in 1993 in half on the basis of the rate at which they have committed crimes, and we call the more frequent half "high-rate offenders" and the other half "low-rate offenders." This even split of the incarcerated population is only for the reference year. Projections of the future under different criminal justice laws allow the split to vary over time. Because high-rate offenders make up a larger fraction of prisoners than of the population on the street, the recidivism rate of persons released from prison exceeds the arrest rate of persons on the street. We used this fact to estimate the ratio of the offense rate of high-rate offenders to that of low-rate offenders.

There are limitations to this modeling framework. Notably, it ignores the chronological age of offenders. A closely related limitation is that we assume criminals' offense rates and their probability of desisting are constant over time (until their criminal careers end completely). One consequence of this is that the model may overestimate the benefits to be gained from the various alternative laws we evaluate. The reason is as follows. High-rate offenders are more likely to be arrested and thus more likely to be sentenced to prison, and, of course, the objective of the three-strike laws is to lock up such offenders. Some high-rate offenders, however, would have become low-rate offenders at some point if they had not been arrested (just as some would have desisted entirely), but our model does not allow for that. The gain from locking up high-rate offenders will thus not be as great as the model predicts.[4] (Of course, some offenders imprisoned while committing crimes at a low rate might have become high-rate offenders. In these cases, the laws deliver a "bonus." Does that make up for the overestimates? No, because the low-rate offenders are not being removed from the street population as fast by the repeat-offender laws.) This bias will, however, affect all sentencing policies analyzed with this model and, thus, is unlikely to greatly affect inferences drawn about the relative efficacy of different sentencing policies, which is the focus of this analysis.

Other Factors Tracked by the Model

Of course, criminals commit different kinds of crime, and penalties are different for different crimes as well. Thus, we keep track of the offense and arrest rates of high- and low-rate offenders by type of crime—violent felonies, felonies that are serious but not violent, and minor felonies.

For some of the minor offenses it is difficult to define the exact number of offenses and, hence, an offending rate. For example, a drug dealer may be almost continually in possession of contraband, and it is impossible to say that the individual committed any particular number of possession-with-intent-to-distribute offenses. Because of this and the fact that people are generally more

---

[4]To put it another way, the model makes it seem as if the alternatives can achieve selective incapacitation more easily than they can.

concerned about serious crimes, we specify offense rates only for serious (including violent) crimes, whereas arrest rates are specified for minor crimes. Also, we express crime prevention benefits in terms of serious crimes averted, not the reduction in all felonies. However, when we discuss index-crime offense rates and serious crimes avoided, we do mean *all* such crime, not just *reported* crime. (We rely on victimization surveys of the general population to obtain data on the total crime rate.)

Once we fully specified the Poisson models, we could construct a simulation that tracks the flows of offenders through different "states" (e.g., boxes in the model). As Figure 3.1 shows, the most important distinctions are whether the individual is free or incarcerated, active or retired. These states alone, however, are not sufficient because sentences sometimes depend on prior records. To preserve the memoryless property of our model, we expanded the number of states tracked to specify the number of previous "strikes" offenders have acquired: zero, one, or two or more.

We ran the simulation model over a 25-year time frame. We chose one year as the time step because it is the most common reporting interval for the data used in the model and provides a convenient metric for reporting results. Appendix E describes in more detail how the model was implemented.

Estimating Costs

As mentioned above, costs are largely influenced by the number of offenders incarcerated; however, the numbers of arrests and trials also affect costs. Each of these factors is an output of the model, and costs are calculated by multiplying those outputs by the factors shown in Table 3.1.

The cost factors are approximations only—gross approximations in the case of the first four lines of the table. The trial costs, for example, are a very rough estimate that does not include losses to government and other employers of citizens who serve on juries. It is important to note, though, that it would take very large errors in the first several cost factors to change the overall thrust of the results, as overall costs turn out to be dominated by prison costs, and prison operating costs in particular (see Section 4).

Our cost analysis does not include an attempt to convert crime reduction benefits into monetary equivalents. These benefits include savings to society from reduced property losses, medical attention, and pain and suffering to victims. The property loss and medical costs associated with the average robbery or assault (the most common types of violent crime) are estimated to be less than

Table 3.1

Criminal Justice System Cost Factors

Cost Item	1993 $
Police cost per arrest[a]	624
Adjudication cost per arrest[b]	1,300
Cost per trial[c]	4,000
Jail operating cost per prisoner-year[d]	10,000
Prison operating cost per prisoner-year[e]	20,800
Prison capital cost per prisoner[e]	97,000

[a]In 1990, the United States at all levels of government spent $31.8 billion on police protection, and made 14.2 million arrests (U.S. Department of Justice, 1992b, pp. 2 and 432). This is $2240 per arrest, or $2500 in 1993 dollars. Assuming that one-fourth of police protection funds are spent on making arrests, we get the estimate of $624 in this table.

[b]In 1990, the United States at all levels of government spent $16.5 billion on "judicial and legal services." This is $1160 per arrest, or $1300 in 1993 dollars (U.S. Department of Justice, 1992b, pp. 2 and 432).

[c]Testimony by Carolyn McIntyre, Legislative Representative, California State Association of Counties, California Senate Appropriations Committee hearing on AB 971 (Jones), March 28, 1994.

[d]Jail operating cost is judged to be approximately half prison operating cost.

[e]Memorandum by Richard S. Welch, Chief, Offender Information Services Branch, California, March 14, 1994, p. 9.

$1000. Depending on how they are estimated, the pain and suffering costs could be much larger. However, the basis for calculating them is not well established.[5]

General Limitations

Aside from the simplifications we have already addressed in regard to constructing the model, our analysis is limited in several ways. Some of the more important ones are as follows.

- We consider only adult, not juvenile, crimes and sanctions. Although juveniles currently account for at least 16 percent of all violent felony arrests, they are not affected by any of the three-strikes laws, and are therefore not included in our analysis.[6]

- The model does not account for the effects of the three-strikes laws on plea bargaining. Some have predicted that many more cases will go to trial under the new law, even accounting for the fact that longer sentences for repeat

[5]A related but more tangible cost is the payments the state makes to victims of crime. These would decrease if crime were reduced. Again, however, these savings would be overwhelmed by the increased prison costs required by the extended-sentence laws.

[6]Juvenile convictions count as strikes, but even this is likely to be challenged as unconstitutional.

offenders would cut down on their offenses, arrests, and trials. However, the latter fact is the only one we consider in the model. (Again, though, because we find that prison costs dominate, even a large error in trial costs is not likely to strongly influence our conclusions about total costs.)

- Because we assume that the initiation rate will be proportional to the general population size, we assume that the fraction of citizens who become active criminals will remain roughly constant over the next 25 years. (Our findings about the differential effects of alternative criminal justice laws do not depend on this growth assumption being more than roughly correct.)

- We assume no deterrent effect. That is, we assume that the various alternatives reduce crime by removing criminals from the streets, not by deterring criminals on the street from committing further crimes. This assumption is consistent with recent research.[7] Nonetheless, we analyzed the sensitivity of our results to the no-deterrence assumption (see Section 4).

- Our specific estimates are for the state of California. Although we hope that our qualitative conclusions and analytical framework are relevant elsewhere, caution should be exercised in generalizing our results to other states, where the characteristics of offenders and sentencing laws may be different.

- We assume that the new three-strikes law will be implemented as written, and we make the same assumption when considering the various alternatives. That is, we assume that sentences will be meted out as directed by the law and enough prison space will be added to keep offenders subject to the new extended sentences locked up for the prescribed periods. We address the potential failure of this assumption in Section 5.

- Our analysis here considers only what expanded incarceration by itself can do to decrease crime. We omit alternative crime-fighting strategies, such as prevention programs or police force expansion. This limitation is very serious in the opinion of some observers of the criminal justice system. We will return to this topic also in Section 5.

---

[7]Blumstein, Cohen, and Nagin (1978); Cook (1980); and MacCoun (1993).

4. Benefits and Costs of the Sentencing Alternatives

Before proceeding to overall crime reduction and cost results, we present one interesting intermediate output of our analysis—the number of FBI index offenses that typical low-rate and high-rate offenders commit in 12 months on the street (see the top panel in Table 4.1). The differences are large. High-rate offenders commit almost 18 times as many crimes as low-rate offenders. The typical high-rate offender commits seven serious crimes per year, including two violent ones. The typical low-rate offender commits one serious crime every two-and-a-half years.[1] Given such differences between criminals, it is easy to see how enhanced repeat-offender penalties can influence the crime rate.

Offense rates, however, are not the same as crime rates. If two persons collaborate in a robbery, each one has committed an offense, but there is only one crime. The bottom two panels of the table show the data that permitted our

Table 4.1

Offenses and Crimes per Offender per Year: Index Felonies, California

Type of Offender	Type of Felony			
	Violent	Serious Only	Other Index	Total Index
Offenses per Offender per Year				
Low-rate	0.12	0.29	0.71	1.11
High-rate	2.03	5.03	12.43	19.49
Offenders per Crime				
Low-rate	1.54	1.79	1.92	1.84
High-rate	1.54	1.79	1.92	1.84
Crimes per Offender per Year				
Low-rate	0.08	0.16	0.37	0.60
High-rate	1.32	2.81	6.47	10.60

NOTE: "Serious only" means "serious but not violent." These are the estimates of offenses per offender per year and offenders per crime by index crime from Table D.5, prorated to violent, serious, and other index crimes using the distributions in Table B.1. The bottom panel in this table is computed from the first two panels. "Other index" crimes include those felonies on the FBI index list, e.g., auto theft, that are not serious. Some felonies, e.g., drug offenses, are not on the index.

---

[1]Recall from Section 3 that we define high- and low-rate offenders by halving the state's incarcerated population in 1993 on the basis of their offense rates. Naturally, other definitions of high- and low-rate offenders would result in different relative offense rates.

18

model to translate reductions in offense rates achieved by locking up criminals into reductions in crime rates.

In presenting our results, we will first compare the Jones three-strikes law with the previous law, as the Jones law is the focus of the current debate. We will then compare the new law with the alternatives defined in Section 2.

Jones Three-Strikes Compared to Previous Law

We estimate that over the next 25 years, the Jones three-strikes law will reduce the annual number of serious crimes in California 28 percent on average below the number that would have been committed under the previous law (see Table 4.2).[2] It will also increase the costs of California's criminal justice system by an average of $5.5 billion a year over the same period.[3] That works out to a 122 percent increase over the $4.5 billion per year estimated for the previous law. (The California Department of Corrections has estimated an annual increase of $5.7 billion.)

By dividing the cost increase by the number of crimes reduced, we arrive at an estimated cost per serious crime prevented of $16,300. This may not be easy to

Table 4.2

Changes in Cost and Serious Crime: Jones Three-Strikes

Item	Previous Law	New Law	Change	Percent Change
Annual cost ($ million)	4,520	10,040	5,520	122
Annual serious crimes (000)	1,219	881	–338	–28
Cost/serious crime prevented ($)		16,300		

NOTE: All figures are discounted at an annual rate of 4 percent.

[2]Although we have not constrained our model to hold the crime *rate* constant under the provisions of the previous law, neither have we introduced factors that would make it vary significantly. As a result, the model results for the previous law show a roughly constant crime rate over the next 25 years, so our reported crime reduction benefits can be read as approximate reductions from the current rate.

[3]The costs and benefits stated here and elsewhere in this report are annualized values (in constant dollars) computed with a 4 percent discount rate. Discounting costs and benefits is standard practice in economic analysis of public programs. It accounts for the fact that a dollar today is more valuable than a dollar 20 years from now because today's dollar can be invested to realize additional earnings or other benefits in the interim. No separate adjustment for inflation is made. Costs may thus be directly compared with costs of other programs in today's dollars. The $5.5 billion difference may be understood as the amount (in constant dollars) that would need to be invested every year to generate, with interest earned, the total discounted 25-year cost difference between the Jones and previous laws. Benefits (crimes prevented) must also be discounted in parallel with discounting of the costs of the alternatives generating those benefits (see Keeler and Cretin, 1983). However, the cost and benefit streams are not strongly skewed over the course of the next 25 years. Thus, most of the annualized discounted costs given in this report approximate the undiscounted constant-dollar amounts the state would actually have to pay in an average year. For the same reason, discounted benefits (crimes prevented) also approximate undiscounted benefits.

conceptualize, given the broad range of crimes covered under the "serious" rubric. Another way to look at it is that each million dollars extra spent under the new three-strikes law will prevent 4 rapes, 11 robberies, 24 aggravated assaults, 22 burglaries of a serious nature, and 1 arson. Every $5 million extra will prevent five times the number of crimes just listed—plus 1 murder.[4]

We thus see that effects on the number of serious crimes will be dominated by decreases in assaults and burglaries (not the murders, rapes, and robberies that many people may believe to be the law's principal targets). How do the costs break down? As shown by Figure 4.1, prison operating and construction costs clearly dominate the cost difference between the new three-strikes law and the previous law. The new law will result in small savings in the costs of arresting and convicting felons and in the cost of jail operation. However, these savings will be overwhelmed by a large difference in prison operating cost and a 12-fold

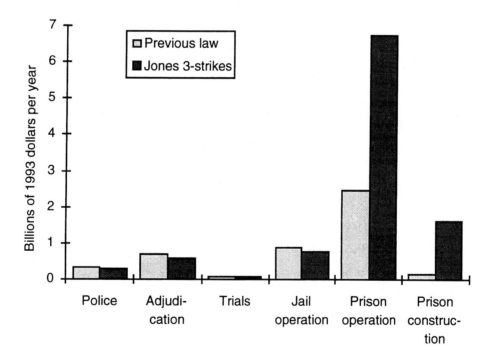

Figure 4.1—Change in Cost by Component: Previous Law Compared to Jones Three-Strikes

---

[4]Our analysis may underestimate the cost to prevent a murder. The reason is that murders are often committed by family members or acquaintances who do not fit the profile of a habitual offender and who thus could not be singled out for incarceration.

The law will also prevent 17 minor burglaries, 32 motor vehicle thefts, and 50 other thefts, plus other crimes not on the FBI index. Because we are primarily interested in serious crimes prevented and we apply the full cost of the law to such crimes, the minor crimes prevented may be viewed as requiring no additional expenditure beyond the $16,300 per serious crime.

increase in the annual cost of prison construction. The extra prison costs result, of course, from the need to build and operate enough additional prison space to accommodate the flow of new prisoners as those subject to the three-strikes law are kept in prison longer. (As explained in Section 3, our trial cost estimates are very limited in scope. However, as is obvious from the graph, even if our trial cost estimates were off by a factor of 5 or 10, the effect on the total cost difference between current and previous laws would not be large.)

Sensitivity of the Results to Changes in Assumptions

Our estimates are, of course, subject to uncertainty. They are uncertain because some of the model inputs cannot be estimated with much accuracy, and because some of the model assumptions are too simple. (Some of these issues were discussed in Section 3.) Although all inputs are consistent with published data, some were estimated in a relatively indirect manner, e.g., offense rates for high-rate and low-rate offenders. We have already mentioned that we do not allow offenders to switch back and forth between high- and low-rate. Also, we did not account for any deterrent effect, i.e., that longer sentences would deter offenders on the street from committing crimes. Researchers have found little to no evidence that such deterrence occurs (Blumstein, Cohen, and Nagin, 1978; Cook, 1980; MacCoun, 1993), but such an effect is alleged by proponents of the new law.[5]

Without assembling a more detailed database and building a more complex model than the resources available for this analysis permitted, we cannot say exactly by how much we may have over- or underestimated crime reduction and cost increases. In lieu of such an effort, we have examined the sensitivity of two of our major conclusions to changes in input parameters. In particular, we have examined the effect of changing two critical assumed values:

1. The ratio of the arrest rate of high-rate offenders to that of low-rate offenders (as a proxy for the ratio of offense rates).

2. The desistance rate of persons with one or more strikes under the Jones law. Increasing this rate is equivalent to changing our assumption of no deterrence. We reason that, if the Jones law were to have a positive deterrent effect, that should show up particularly among persons with strikes.

---

[5]Some evidence suggests the existence of a deterrent effect from increasing the *probability* that a felon will serve time (of whatever length).

We increased and decreased the ratio of the arrest rate (number of arrests per year out of prison) of high-rate offenders to low-rate offenders by 25 percent, and we increased and decreased the desistance rate of offenders with one or more strikes under the Jones bill by 25 percent. The first of these has the effect of changing the ease with which a repeat-offender law can single out high-rate offenders and thus affect the crime rate. The second (in the positive direction) is equivalent to an assumption that the Jones law will each year cause one of every 40 felons with strikes to desist.

In each case, we calculated the relative reduction in crime rate brought about by the Jones law under the given assumptions, and the relative increase in the average prison population, the main driver for costs. We then compared these changes to those under our standard assumptions, as reflected in the results shown in Table 4.2. Table 4.3 displays the differences between the two sets of results.

As Table 4.3 shows, none of our sensitivity cases affected our estimate of the decrease in crime rate or increase in prison population by more than 10 percent in absolute value. At one extreme, if high- and low-rate offenders are "25 percent more different" than we assumed, and if the Jones bill increases desistance by 25 percent, the decrease in crime rate will be larger by about 6 percent and the increase in prison population will be about 7 percent smaller. This means, for example, that the crime rate reduction will be the standard 28 percent times 106 percent, or 30 percent (*not* 28 percent *plus* 6 percent). At the other extreme, the decrease in crime rate will be smaller by about 8 percent and the increase in the prison population will be larger by about 10 percent.

There may be other sources of error. It is possible that varying other assumptions might show somewhat larger effects, and there are minor differences between the model inputs and the laws (see Appendix C). Taking all this into account, we believe that the estimates presented here can be viewed as accurate to within one-fifth (20 percent). For example, when Table 4.2 reports that the Jones three-strikes law will reduce crime by 28 percent, this may be interpreted as a reduction of at least 23 percent but no more than 34 percent.

Given that the cost estimates are driven by prison costs, and that the prison cost factors we use should be quite reliable, our costs should not vary more than we expect our projected prison population to vary. Thus, again, these may be regarded as correct to within 20 percent. That is, the extra cost of the Jones three-

Table 4.3

Sensitivity of Crime Rate and Prison Population to Assumptions

Assumption (relative to standard)		Relative Difference in	
Arrest Rate of High-Rate Offenders Divided by Arrest Rate of Low-Rate Offenders	Desistance Rate of Offenders with 1 or More Strikes Under the Jones Law	Decrease in Crime Rate	Increase in Prison Pop.
25% lower	25% lower	–7.5%	+9.6%
25% lower	No change	–2.8%	+2.2%
25% lower	25% higher	+1.4%	–4.0%
No change	25% lower	–4.6%	+6.8%
No change	No change	0.0%	0.0%
No change	25% higher	+4.0%	–5.9%
25% higher	25% lower	–2.3%	+4.7%
25% higher	No change	+2.2%	–1.7%
25% higher	25% higher	+6.1%	–7.3%

NOTE: Negative results in column 3 indicate smaller decreases in crime, i.e., higher crime rates; positive results, vice-versa. Results in columns 3 and 4 are percent of change under standard assumptions, *not percent of results under previous law* (see the text).

strikes law should fall within the range extending from $4.5 billion to $6.5 billion annually.

Trends

Reporting average annual results, as we have done so far, obscures differences in crimes prevented and cost increases over time. We project that the number of serious and violent crimes prevented each year will increase rapidly during the new law's first ten years, then more slowly thereafter (Figure 4.2).

As mentioned in Section 3, the major determinant of crime rates is the number of offenders on the street—particularly high-rate offenders. Figure 4.3 shows how much the Jones three-strikes law is expected to reduce the number of high-rate offenders on the street over the 25-year projection period. Again, note the big change early in the period, culminating after several years in a drop of about one-third from the previous-law projection. No graph of the effect on low-rate offenders is presented because the projections under the two laws are so close that the lines virtually overlap. Low-rate offenders will be little affected by the new law because their low rate of committing crimes means a low rate of accumulating strikes, and consequently a low probability of receiving the enhanced sanctions under the second- and third-strike provisions.

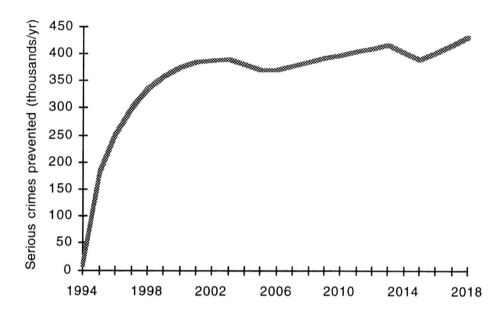

Figure 4.2—Serious Crimes Prevented by Year: Jones Three-Strikes Law

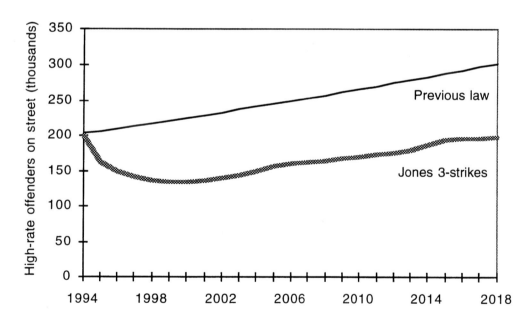

Figure 4.3—High-Rate Offenders on Street by Year: Jones Three-Strikes Compared to
Previous Law

The additional costs under the new law (Figure 4.4) will fluctuate considerably over time because of the on-again off-again nature of the need to add prison spaces. We estimate, for example, that actual time incarcerated for a serious crime on second strike will go up to about ten years under the new law. It was roughly three years under the previous law.[6] Thus, those convicted of their second serious felony in 1992 will be getting out of prison sometime around 1995; those convicted in 1993, around 1996. Second-strikers convicted in 1994 will not emerge until about 2004. When coupled with the immediate effects of sending all serious felons to prison, the Jones law's second-strike sentence increases will result in a buildup of prisoners and prison costs, relative to the previous law, until 2004.[7] Then, the first second-strikers convicted under the Jones law will be released and costs will drop for a while on a relative basis. Meanwhile, extra costs associated with third-strikers will be increasing until those prisoners begin coming out in 2014. (The effects of these 10-year and 20-year prisoner releases also show up in a minor way in the crime reduction curve in Figure 4.2.)

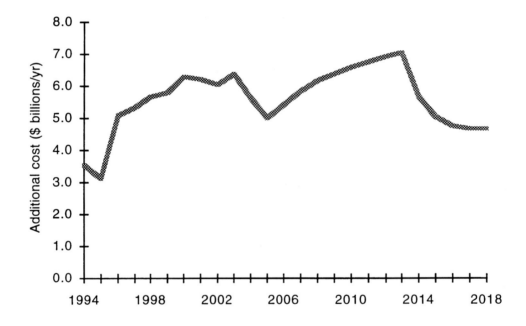

Figure 4.4—Additional Cost per Year: Jones Three-Strikes Law

---

[6]This applies only to those who were sentenced to prison. Jones provides for a doubling of sentence on second strike, but it also cuts good time from 50 percent to 20 percent maximum. The effect is thus to more than triple the current actual time incarcerated for those imprisoned for a second serious offense.

[7]We count the full capital cost for adding prison space in the year the space is needed.

Figure 4.5 compares the projected number of prison spaces under the Jones three-strikes law with those expected if the previous law had remained unchanged. Over most of the 25-year projection period, the Jones three-strikes law will more than double the required number of prison spaces. Again, flexes in the curve are apparent around 2004 and 2014.

Comparison with Alternative Laws

We now compare the crime reduction and extra costs anticipated as a result of the Jones three-strikes law with those of several alternatives. These comparisons are in the form of crimes prevented and extra costs incurred relative to the previous law. Results are given in Table 4.4 and discussed through the graphical presentations in the remainder of this section.

First, as might be expected, the less restrictive alternatives would generally reduce crime by a smaller amount than the Jones three-strikes law (see Figure 4.6). However, the second-strike-only alternative would achieve 85 percent of the Jones law's crime reduction benefit. Because the two options are identical except for the third-strike provisions, this implies that only 15 percent of the new law's effect will result from those provisions. This is ironic, considering the emphasis on the third-strike penalties in much of the public debate on the law.

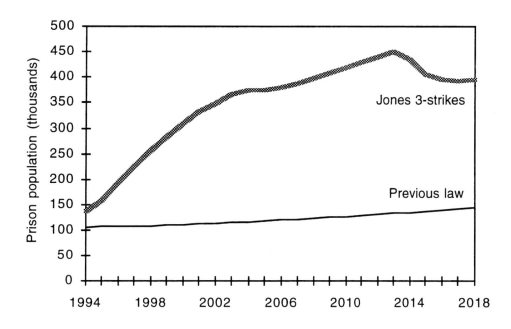

Figure 4.5—Projected Prison Populations by Year: Jones Three-Strikes Compared to Previous Law

26

Table 4.4

Summary Cost-Benefit Comparison of Alternative Laws

Item	Previous Law	Alternative	Change	Percent Change
Jones Three-Strikes				
Annual cost (millions)	$4,520	$10,040	$5,520	122%
Annual serious crimes (000)	1,219	881	–338	–28%
Cost/serious crime prevented		$16,300		
Jones Second-Strike Only				
Annual cost (millions)	$4,520	$8,600	$4,080	90%
Annual serious crimes (000)	1,219	932	–287	–24%
Cost/serious crime prevented		$14,200		
Jones Violent Only				
Annual cost (millions)	$4,520	$7,100	$2,580	57%
Annual serious crimes (000)	1,219	999	–220	–18%
Cost/serious crime prevented		$11,800		
Rainey Three-Strikes				
Annual cost (millions)	$4,520	$8,510	$3,990	88%
Annual serious crimes (000)	1,219	952	–267	–22%
Cost/serious crime prevented		$14,900		
Guaranteed Full Term				
Annual cost (millions)	$4,520	$8,920	$4,400	97%
Annual serious crimes (000)	1,219	877	–342	–28%
Cost/serious crime prevented		$12,900		

NOTE: All figures are discounted at an annual rate of 4 percent.

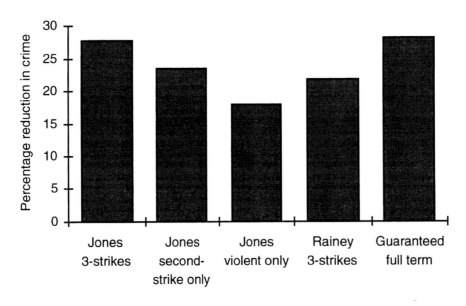

Figure 4.6—Percentage Reduction in Serious Crime from Jones Three-Strikes Compared to Alternatives

The Jones violent-only alternative retains the third-strike provision but invokes second- or third-strike sentencing sanctions only for violent crimes. That alternative would not be as effective as the second-strike-only alternative, but it would still achieve two-thirds of the crime reduction benefit of the Jones law.

The Rainey three-strikes bill is also more focused on violent offenders, but is harsher not only to them but also to third-strike serious nonviolent offenders. It is more lenient than the Jones law on second-strike serious, nonviolent offenders and much more lenient on one- and two-strikers with an additional minor felony conviction. The result of these differences is that the crime reduction benefit would be less, and would also be less than that of the Jones law without the third-strike provision.

The guaranteed-full-term alternative matches the Jones three-strikes law in crime reduction. Recall that the full-term alternative contains no second- or third-strike provisions. It simply requires that all offenders convicted of a serious felony serve in prison the full sentence given to them. It would achieve the full effect of the Jones law even though it would cut in half the fraction of offenders convicted of a minor felony who go to prison—from 21 percent to 11 percent. The Jones law will *increase* this proportion for those who have at least one strike to 100 percent. This latter point provides a clue as to how the crime reduction power of a three-strikes law, supposedly targeted to keep violent repeat offenders incarcerated, could be matched by a no-strikes alternative. In fact, the Jones law is *not* targeted toward violent repeat offenders. Forty percent of the crimes that would cause a strike to accumulate are burglaries, and the chance that the third strike that sends someone to prison for life will be a *minor* felony is better than even.

The costs of most of the alternatives follow the benefits (Figure 4.7). However, the savings relative to the Jones three-strikes cost would be greater for all other alternatives on a percentage basis than the reduction in benefits. This is shown more directly in Figure 4.8, which displays cost per serious crime prevented. By this criterion, the Jones violent-only alternative would be best; it would deliver two-thirds the benefit of the Jones three-strikes at only half the cost, for a cost per serious crime averted of about $12,000, compared to roughly $16,000 for the new law. This alternative is more cost-effective than the Jones law for two reasons. First, it spends less money locking up late-career offenders who might soon give up on crime anyway. Second, it spends less money locking up late-career *low-rate* offenders, who are disproportionately affected by the Jones law's counting a minor felony as a third strike.

28

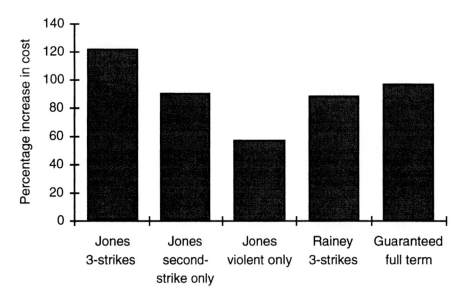

Figure 4.7—Percentage Increase in Cost from Jones Three-Strikes Compared to
Alternatives

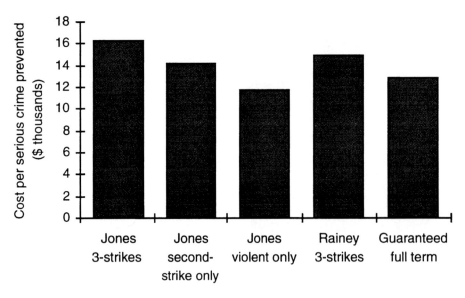

Figure 4.8—Cost per Serious Crime Prevented from Jones Three-Strikes
and Alternatives

Because the Jones second-strike alternative falls between the Jones law and the
violent-only alternative in number of late-career criminals affected, it also falls
between the two in cost-effectiveness. Again, this alternative permits a separate
evaluation of the new law's third strike. The bill for the law's other provisions is
the same as that for the second strike-only alternative: about $14,000 for each
serious crime prevented. The cost of the third strike is twice as much per serious

crime prevented, again reflecting the inefficiency of late-career lockups and charging a third strike for a minor felony.

The guaranteed-full-term alternative puts more emphasis on incapacitating offenders early in their criminal careers—it gives short prison sentences to many who are given none by Jones instead of giving long sentences to a few. It requires that even first-time serious felons serve full terms in prison and saves some of the money that the new law spends locking up those convicted of minor felonies. By doing so, the full-term alternative would achieve a cost-effectiveness ratio second only to that of the violent-only.

We do not wish, however, to establish cost per serious crime prevented as a touchstone criterion. The point, after all, is to reduce crime (some would say as much as possible), and the various alternatives are limited in how much they can achieve. Although it is true that the violent-only alternative can achieve two-thirds the benefit of the Jones three-strikes law at half the expense, one cannot achieve the entire benefit by putting more money into that approach.

The guaranteed-full-term alternative thus stands out for its ability to realize the full benefit of the new three-strikes law at somewhat less cost. (This is graphically represented in Figure 4.9.) However, both the new law and all the

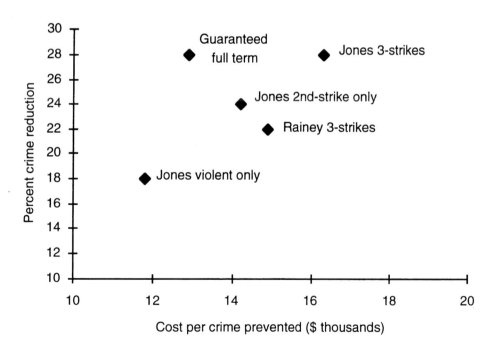

Figure 4.9—Benefits and Cost-Effectiveness from Jones Three-Strikes Compared to Alternatives

alternatives, even the Jones violent-only, represent major increases in spending over current levels. In the next section, we try to gain some perspective on the implications of such expenditures within California's current and prospective budgetary environment.

5. Footing the Bill

We have estimated that, over the next 25 years, the Jones three-strikes law will prevent on the order of 340,000 serious crimes per year in California at an additional cost of roughly $5.5 billion annually, or about $16,000 per serious crime prevented. Alternatively, the guaranteed-full-term alternative could prevent the same number of serious crimes for an additional expenditure of about $4.4 billion annually, or a cost of about $13,000 per crime prevented.

This analysis cannot determine whether it is "worth it" to increase California's criminal justice budget by such large amounts to achieve a 28 percent reduction in serious crimes (mostly burglaries and assaults) committed by adults. That determination depends on subjective factors that are difficult to quantify. However, some perspective can be gained on the issue of "worth" by asking two questions: First, are there other ways in which $5.5 billion per year could be spent that would reduce crime by more than 28 percent? Second, what must be given up to spend an additional $5.5 billion annually on crime reduction?

How Else Could the Money Be Spent to Reduce Crime?

We restrict ourselves here to two often-mentioned alternatives: increasing police protection and attacking the causes of crime. We cannot assess the value of these alternative expenditures relative to the new three-strikes law, but we can frame the comparison in a way that perhaps allows some perspective.

Governments ranging from local to federal have been attempting to increase the size of police forces. In Los Angeles, for example, the mayor hopes to find money for a major expansion of the police department. The financially strapped city may have to settle for a more modest buildup, but even the mayor's plan would increase the police force by less than 50 percent. The new federal crime law aims to add 100,000 police across the country—a gain of less than 20 percent. Five and a half billion dollars is on the same order of magnitude as what California spends annually on law enforcement at all levels. By redirecting that amount of money from implementing the Jones three-strikes law to funding police protection, California could thus *double* the number of police officers in *every* jurisdiction in the state. Alternatively, a somewhat smaller expansion could be undertaken in exchange for higher police pay, which might result in a force that is not only bigger but one with higher morale and greater aptitude.

32

In recent years, law enforcement officials have stressed that they can make only so much headway against crime if the root causes are not addressed. The reasons for this are clear: Our analysis suggests that there may be as many as one million felons on the street in California. At some point, these individuals will stop committing crimes and will be replaced by another million felons. The typical criminal career lasts roughly a decade. This implies that something on the order of a million California children under the age of ten will become felons. The new three-strikes law does little or nothing to change that prospect (and neither would the alternatives evaluated in Section 4). It works by transferring felons from the street to prison; it does not act to shut off the supply.

The root causes of much serious crime are well known. They include broken families, dysfunctional families, poverty, sociopathic inclinations, the drug culture. Can money spent combatting these causes be as effective as the three-strikes law? To be so, $5.5 billion would have to persuade 28,000 children who would have become felons not to take up a criminal career.[1] The question can thus be rephrased: Can $5.5 million be targeted to environments in which children have a high propensity for crime in such a way as to keep 28 children who would otherwise have become criminals from doing so?

What Must Be Given Up to Fund Three Strikes?

Further insight can be gained into whether the Jones law is worth $5.5 billion a year if we ask whether Californians are willing to give up that much in other services. This is a more basic question than the preceding one, as it asks whether Californians want to shift large amounts of current spending to *any* criminal justice endeavor.

We begin with the assumption that higher taxes are unlikely. In particular, three strikes costs enough that the additional tax required to fund it would not be small—probably at least $300 per year from the average working person. Borrowing would also appear to be out of the question, given recent reactions from the bond rating services and the electorate, not to mention the impracticality of borrowing as a long-term source of revenue.

But the state will have difficulty deciding what current spending should be reduced to make room for three strikes. Figure 5.1 shows how state spending is

---

[1] Over the long run, the Jones law's effectiveness can be equaled if 28 percent of those who would have become felons are persuaded not to. One year's share of the million felons replaced every ten years is 100,000. Twenty-eight percent of that is 28,000.

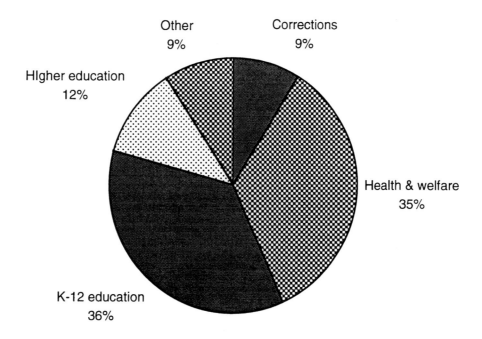

Figure 5.1—Distribution of California General-Fund Appropriations, FY94

currently allocated.[2] By 2002, the new three-strikes law will require an additional 9 percentage-point increase in the fraction of the state budget devoted to corrections, now at 9 percent.[3] Where will those 9 percentage points come from? They cannot come from K–12 education. Proposition 98, written into the state constitution by California voters, sets minimal levels of funding for K–12 education. Because school enrollment will grow faster than the tax base, the percentage of the budget devoted to K–12 education will have to *increase* from the current 36 to 47 by 2002.

Health and welfare are also unlikely sources of funds. This portion of the budget has been increasing for 25 years and its share of the general fund is now 7 percentage points higher than it was in 1969. If the state wants federal assistance in funding Aid to Families with Dependent Children and MediCal (California's version of Medicaid), the state must provide its own share of the funds needed to support beneficiaries meeting federal entitlement criteria. Like

---

[2]We are grateful to RAND colleague Stephen J. Carroll for allowing us to use his analysis of current and future state expenditures; that analysis is part of an ongoing research project.

[3]This assumes relatively optimistic growth in money available for the general fund (nearly 50 percent between FY94 and FY02, in constant dollars). The growth in the Corrections budget is based on growth in the entire pre-Jones budget at a rate equal to that anticipated for prison construction and operation under the previous law (roughly 10 percent in constant dollars over the eight years). The extra three-strikes prison costs are then added to that.

school enrollment, the number of beneficiaries is expected to grow faster than California's population as a whole, so health and welfare spending will also increase as a percentage of the state's budget.

That leaves higher education and other government expenditures. Higher education's share of the budget has already fallen from 17 percent to 12 percent in the last 25 years. The result has been sharp increases in out-of-pocket costs for students and substantial cuts in the availability of classes.

Other government expenditures support a broad range of services such as pollution control, park and other natural resource management, workplace safety assurance, and insurance industry regulation. These services have also fallen as a percentage of total state expenditures—from 12 percent in 1980 to 9 percent now.

Although state funding for higher education and other government services has been falling, these are the only practical sources of funds for the three-strikes law. To support implementation of the law, total spending for higher education and other services would have to fall by more than 40 percent over the next eight years. At the same time, these spending categories will face severe pressure from the increasing health, welfare, and K–12 education mandates (for the combined effect of three strikes and K–12, see Figure 5.2). Increases in expenditures on corrections have tripled its portion of the state budget since 1980. If the three-strikes law remains in place, by 2002 the state government will be spending more money keeping people in prison than putting people through college. This allocation of funds raises questions of values that cannot be settled through analysis. Instead, they will be settled in November by the electorate when it decides whether three strikes is a good long-term strategy for the state.

Practical Considerations

Throughout this report, we have assumed that the Jones three-strikes law (or an alternative) will be implemented as written. It is clear from the preceding discussion, however, that something's got to give. Even if Californians pass the three-strikes initiative, they are unlikely to accept the state government's abdicating large portions of what they see as its responsibility for higher education, environmental quality, and so on. Legislators who found it politically attractive to vote for the three-strikes law may find it politically unattractive to fully fund its implementation. Voters may balk at the billions of dollars in additional prison bonds that will have to be passed in the coming years.

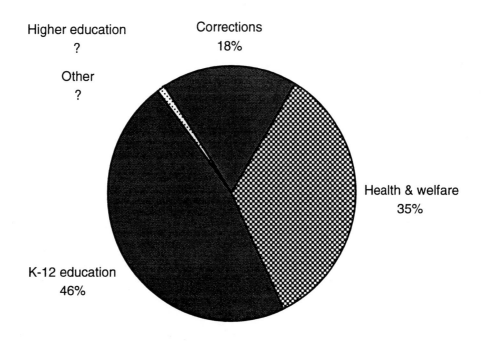

Assumes no increase in health & welfare (unlikely).

Figure 5.2—Budgetary Squeeze on Higher Education and Other Services, FY02

The results of underfunding the law are difficult to predict. If prison space is insufficient, courts may order the early release of prisoners. If they try to follow the spirit of the Jones law, they may release those with a brief record in favor of retaining older criminals behind bars. This may not be the right choice from the point of view of crime reduction, as younger criminals may have more of a criminal career ahead of them than older ones. On the other hand, prosecutors and judges, who are also politically accountable to the public, may choose to apply the law selectively. In the months since the three-strikes law took effect, the media have reported instances of rebellion against the law within the judicial system. This may continue as judges, prosecutors, witnesses, and juries have to face the possibility that criminals without a history of violence would be given long prison sentences.[4]

Clearly, failure to fully implement the law will decrease both its costs and its crime reduction benefits. Though these reductions should occur in similar

---

[4]It is ironic that the sweeping changes required by the three-strikes law, combined with its near-prohibitive cost, may require legislators and criminal justice officials and practitioners to make the very kind of discretionary choices that proponents of the initiative were trying to take away from them.

proportions, their magnitude is uncertain. Only time and the workings of the criminal justice system will reveal the extent to which the new three-strikes law will realize the benefits Californians expect from it—and the costs many of them do not.

Appendix
A. The Jones Three-Strikes Law

We reproduce here the text of AB 971, California's current law establishing penalties for repeat offenders. Known as the Jones three-strikes law, after the bill's principal author and the popular slogan, the bill was passed by the California legislature and was signed by Governor Pete Wilson in March 1994. It is almost identical to the text of Proposition 184 on the statewide November ballot. If Proposition 184 passes, it would supersede the Jones law but would have little practical effect on the penal code. However, because it is an initiative, it could be repealed only by initiative, and any amendments by the legislature would have to be in furtherance of the initiative's purpose (and would have to survive any court challenges alleging they are not). If the proposition fails, the Jones law would continue in force, subject to legislative modification.

BILL NUMBER: AB 971   CHAPTERED 03/07/94

BILL TEXT

CHAPTER 12

FILED WITH SECRETARY OF STATE   MARCH 7, 1994
APPROVED BY GOVERNOR   MARCH 7, 1994
PASSED THE ASSEMBLY   MARCH 3, 1994
PASSED THE SENATE   JANUARY 31, 1994
AMENDED IN ASSEMBLY   JANUARY 26, 1994
AMENDED IN ASSEMBLY   JANUARY 13, 1994
AMENDED IN ASSEMBLY   JANUARY 3, 1994
AMENDED IN ASSEMBLY   APRIL 12, 1993

INTRODUCED BY Assembly Members Jones and Costa

(Principal coauthors: Senators Wyman and Presley) (Coauthors: Assembly Members Aguiar, Allen, Alpert, Andal, Boland, Bowler, Bronshvag, Valerie Brown, Brulte, Bustamante, Conroy, Epple, Escutia, Ferguson, Goldsmith, Harvey, Haynes, Hoge, Horcher, Johnson, Morrow, Mountjoy, Nolan, O'Connell, Polanco, Pringle, Quackenbush, Richter, Seastrand, Takasugi, Umberg, Weggeland, and Woodruff)

(Coauthors: Senators Boatwright, Hurtt, and McCorquodale)

MARCH 1, 1993

An act to amend Section 667 of the Penal Code, relating to sentencing, and declaring the urgency thereof, to take effect immediately.

LEGISLATIVE COUNSEL'S DIGEST

AB 971, Jones. Sentencing: prior felony convictions. (1) Existing law, added by initiative statute, provides, among other things, that any person who is convicted of a serious felony, as defined, and who has been previously convicted of a serious felony in California, or of any offense committed in another jurisdiction which includes all of the elements of a serious felony, shall receive, in addition to the sentence imposed for the present felony, a 5-year enhancement for each prior felony conviction on charges brought and tried separately.

This bill would declare the intent of the Legislature to ensure longer prison sentences and greater punishment for those who commit a felony and have been previously convicted of serious and/or violent felony offenses.

This bill would, in addition, provide that in addition to any other enhancement or penalty provisions that may apply, (1) if a defendant has one prior felony conviction, as defined, the determinate term, or minimum term for an indeterminate term, shall be twice the term otherwise provided as punishment for the current conviction, (2) if a defendant has 2 or more prior convictions, the term for the current felony conviction shall be an indeterminate term of imprisonment in the state prison for life with a minimum term of the indeterminate term as the greatest of (a) 3 times the term otherwise provided as punishment for each current felony conviction subsequent to the 2 or more prior felony convictions, (b) imprisonment in the state prison for 25 years, or (c) the term determined by the court for the underlying conviction, including any applicable enhancement or punishment provisions.

The bill would also provide, among other things, that probation shall not be granted nor shall the execution or imposition of sentence be suspended if the defendant has a prior felony conviction.

(2) The bill would declare that it is to take effect immediately as an urgency statute.

THE PEOPLE OF THE STATE OF CALIFORNIA DO ENACT AS FOLLOWS:

SECTION 1. Section 667 of the Penal Code is amended to read:

667. (a)　　　(1) In compliance with subdivision (b) of Section 1385, any person convicted of a serious felony who previously has been convicted of a serious felony in this state or of any offense committed in another jurisdiction which includes all of the elements of any serious felony, shall receive, in addition to the sentence imposed by the court for the present offense, a five-year enhancement for each such prior conviction on charges brought and tried separately. The terms of the present offense and each enhancement shall run consecutively.

　　　(2) This subdivision shall not be applied when the punishment imposed under other provisions of law would result in a longer term of imprisonment. There is no requirement of prior incarceration or commitment for this subdivision to apply.

　　　(3) The Legislature may increase the length of the enhancement of sentence provided in this subdivision by a statute passed by majority vote of each house thereof.

　　　(4) As used in this subdivision, "serious felony" means a serious felony listed in subdivision (c) of Section 1192.7.

　　　(5) This subdivision shall not apply to a person convicted of selling, furnishing, administering, or giving, or offering to sell, furnish, administer, or give to a minor any methamphetamine-related drug or any precursors of methamphetamine unless the prior conviction was for a serious felony described in subparagraph (24) of subdivision (c) of Section 1192.7.

(b) It is the intent of the Legislature in enacting subdivisions (b) to (i), inclusive, to ensure longer prison sentences and greater punishment for those who commit a felony and have been previously convicted of serious and/or violent felony offenses.

(c) Notwithstanding any other law, if a defendant has been convicted of a felony and it has been pled and proved that the defendant has one or more prior felony convictions as defined in subdivision (d), the court shall adhere to each of the following:

　　　(1) There shall not be an aggregate term limitation for purposes of consecutive sentencing for any subsequent felony conviction.

　　　(2) Probation for the current offense shall not be granted, nor shall execution or imposition of the sentence be suspended for any prior offense.

(3) The length of time between the prior felony conviction and the current felony conviction shall not affect the imposition of sentence.

(4) There shall not be a commitment to any other facility other than the state prison. Diversion shall not be granted nor shall the defendant be eligible for commitment to the California Rehabilitation Center as provided in Article 2 (commencing with Section 3050) of Chapter 1 of Division 3 of the Welfare and Institutions Code.

(5) The total amount of credits awarded pursuant to Article 2.5 (commencing with Section 2930) of Chapter 7 of Title 1 of Part 3 shall not exceed one-fifth of the total term of imprisonment imposed and shall not accrue until the defendant is physically placed in the state prison.

(6) If there is a current conviction for more than one felony count not committed on the same occasion, and not arising from the same set of operative facts, the court shall sentence the defendant consecutively on each count pursuant to subdivision (e).

(7) If there is a current conviction for more than one serious or violent felony as described in paragraph (6), the court shall impose the sentence for each conviction consecutive to the sentence for any other conviction for which the defendant may be consecutively sentenced in the manner prescribed by law.

(8) Any sentence imposed pursuant to subdivision (e) will be imposed consecutive to any other sentence which the defendant is already serving, unless otherwise provided by law.

(d) Notwithstanding any other law and for the purposes of subdivisions (b) to (i), inclusive, a prior conviction of a felony shall be defined as:

(1) Any offense defined in subdivision (c) of Section 667.5 as a violent felony or any offense defined in subdivision (c) of Section 1192.7 as a serious felony in this state. The determination of whether a prior conviction is a prior felony conviction for purposes of subdivisions (b) to (i), inclusive, shall be made upon the date of that prior conviction and is not affected by the sentence imposed unless the sentence automatically, upon the initial sentencing, converts the felony to a misdemeanor. None of the following dispositions shall affect the determination that a prior conviction is a prior felony for purposes of subdivisions (b) to (i), inclusive:

(A) The suspension of imposition of judgment or sentence.

(B) The stay of execution of sentence.

(C) The commitment to the State Department of Health Services as a mentally disordered sex offender following a conviction of a felony.

(D) The commitment to the California Rehabilitation Center or any other facility whose function is rehabilitative diversion from the state prison.

(2) A conviction in another jurisdiction for an offense that, if committed in California, is punishable by imprisonment in the state prison. A prior conviction of a particular felony shall include a conviction in another jurisdiction for an offense that includes all of the elements of the particular felony as defined in subdivision (c) of Section 667.5 or subdivision (c) of Section 1192.7.

(3) A prior juvenile adjudication shall constitute a prior felony conviction for purposes of sentence enhancement if:

(A) The juvenile was 16 years of age or older at the time he or she committed the prior offense.

(B) The prior offense is listed in subdivision (b) of Section 707 of the Welfare and Institutions Code or described in paragraph (1) or (2) as a felony.

(C) The juvenile was found to be a fit and proper subject to be dealt with under the juvenile court law.

(D) The juvenile was adjudged a ward of the juvenile court within the meaning of Section 602 of the Welfare and Institutions Code because the person committed an offense listed in subdivision (b) of Section 707 of the Welfare and Institutions Code.

(e) For purposes of subdivisions (b) to (i), inclusive, and in addition to any other enhancement or punishment provisions which may apply, the following shall apply where a defendant has a prior felony conviction:

(1) If a defendant has one prior felony conviction that has been pled and proved, the determinate term or minimum term for an indeterminate term shall be twice the term otherwise provided as punishment for the current felony conviction.

(2) (A) If a defendant has two or more prior felony convictions as defined in subdivision (d) that have been pled and proved, the term for the current felony conviction shall be an indeterminate term of life imprisonment with a minimum term of the indeterminate sentence calculated as the greater of:

(i) Three times the term otherwise provided as punishment for each current felony conviction subsequent to the two or more prior felony convictions.

(ii) Imprisonment in the state prison for 25 years.

(iii) The term determined by the court pursuant to Section 1170 for the underlying conviction, including any enhancement applicable under Chapter 4.5 (commencing with Section 1170) of Title 7 of Part 2, or any period prescribed by Section 190 or 3046.

(B) The indeterminate term described in subparagraph (A) shall be served consecutive to any other term of imprisonment for which a consecutive term may be imposed by law. Any other term imposed subsequent to any indeterminate term described in subparagraph (A) shall not be merged therein but shall commence at the time the person would otherwise have been released from prison.

(f)   (1) Notwithstanding any other law, subdivisions (b) to (i), inclusive, shall be applied in every case in which a defendant has a prior felony conviction as defined in subdivision (d). The prosecuting attorney shall plead and prove each prior felony conviction except as provided in paragraph (2).

(2) The prosecuting attorney may move to dismiss or strike a prior felony conviction allegation in the furtherance of justice pursuant to Section 1385, or if there is insufficient evidence to prove the prior conviction. If upon the satisfaction of the court that there is insufficient evidence to prove the prior felony conviction, the court may dismiss or strike the allegation.

(g) Prior felony convictions shall not be used in plea bargaining as defined in subdivision (b) of Section 1192.7. The prosecution shall plead and prove all known prior felony convictions and shall not enter into any agreement to strike or seek the dismissal of any prior felony conviction allegation except as provided in paragraph (2) of subdivision (f).

(h) All references to existing statutes in subdivisions (c) to (g), inclusive, are to statutes as they existed on June 30, 1993.

(i) If any provision of subdivisions (b) to (h), inclusive, or the application thereof to any person or circumstance is held invalid, that invalidity shall not affect other provisions or applications of those subdivisions which can be given effect without the invalid provision or application, and to this end the provisions of those subdivisions are severable.

(j) The provisions of this section shall not be amended by the Legislature except by statute passed in each house by rollcall vote entered in the journal, two-thirds of the membership concurring, or by a statute that becomes effective only when approved by the electors.

SEC. 2. This act is an urgency statute necessary for the immediate preservation of the public peace, health, or safety within the meaning of Article IV of the Constitution and shall go into immediate effect. The facts constituting the necessity are:

In order to ensure longer prison sentences and greater punishment for those who commit a felony and have been previously convicted of serious or violent felony offenses, and to protect the public from the imminent threat posed by those repeat felony offenders, it is necessary that this act take effect immediately.

B. Classification of Crimes as Serious or Violent

In this appendix, we take two approaches to conveying the nature of serious and violent crimes. First, we list the crimes, with reference to sections in the penal code. Second, we compare California's serious and violent categories to the FBI index categories from the bureau's Uniform Crime Reports.

Definition of Violent Felonies

The following felonies are identified as violent in California Penal Code Section 667.8.

1. Murder or voluntary manslaughter

2. Mayhem

3. Rape, in violation of Penal Code Section 261(2)

4. Sodomy by force, violence, duress, menace, or fear of immediate and unlawful bodily injury on the victim or another person

5. Oral copulation by force, violence, duress, menace, or fear of immediate and unlawful bodily injury on the victim or another person

6. Lewd acts on a child under 14 in violation of Penal Code Section 288

7. Any felony punishable by death or imprisonment in the state prison for life

8. Any felony in which the defendant inflicts great bodily injury (except on an accomplice) pursuant to Penal Code Section 12022.7 or uses a firearm pursuant to Penal Code Section 12022.5

9. First degree burglary (inhabited dwelling etc.) plus Penal Code 12022(b)

10. Arson in violation of Penal Code 451(a)

11. Rape by force, violence, duress, menace or fear of immediate and unlawful bodily injury on the victim or another person

12. Attempted murder

13. A violation of Penal Code 12308, explosion with intent to murder

Definition of Serious Felonies

The following felonies are identified as serious in California Penal Code Section 1192.7.

1. Murder or voluntary manslaughter

2. Mayhem

3. Rape, in violation of Penal Code Section 261(2)

4. Sodomy by force, violence, duress, menace, or fear of immediate and unlawful bodily injury on the victim or another person

5. Oral copulation by force, violence, duress, menace, or fear of immediate and unlawful bodily injury on the victim or another person

6. Lewd acts on a child under 14 in violation of Penal Code Section 288

7. Any felony punishable by death or imprisonment in the state prison for life

8. Any felony in which the defendant inflicts great bodily injury (except on an accomplice) pursuant to Penal Code Section 12022.7 or uses a firearm pursuant to Penal Code Section 12022.5

9. Attempted murder

10. Assault with intent to commit rape or robbery

11. Assault with a deadly weapon or instrument on a peace officer

12. Assault by a life prisoner on a non-inmate

13. Assault with a deadly weapon by an inmate

14. Arson

15. Exploding a destructive device or any explosive with intent to injure

16. Exploding a destructive device or any explosive causing great bodily injury

17. Exploding a destructive device or any explosive with intent to murder

18. Burglary of an inhabited dwelling house, or trailer coach as defined by the Vehicle Code, or inhabited portion of any other building

19. Robbery or bank robbery

20. Kidnapping

Comparison with FBI Index Categories

In Table B.1, we quantify the allocation of FBI index crimes to California's serious and violent categories. Table and page references below are to California Department of Justice (1992a).

Table B.1

Relation of FBI Index Crimes to Crimes Defined by California as Serious or Violent

| FBI Index Crime | Percent Classified by California as | | |
	Violent	Serious Only	Neither
Murder	100	0	0
Rape	80	20	0
Robbery	40	60	0
Assault	50	50	0
Burglary	0	60	40
Theft	0	0	100
MVT	0	0	100
Arson	5	95	0

NOTE: Estimated by the authors from detailed lists of crimes included in each FBI index crime category, and detailed lists of crimes included in each California crime category. "Serious only" means "serious but not violent." MVT is motor vehicle theft.

Murder and manslaughter are both classified as violent.

Rapes in violation of Penal Code 261(2) (i.e., by force, violence, duress, menace, or fear of immediate bodily injury on the victim or another person) are defined as violent. Rapes defined as serious but not violent include those in which the victim is drunk or otherwise insensate and those in which the perpetrator is a spouse. (Statutory rapes are excluded from the FBI index category.) The fraction of rapes that are "rapes by force" has increased steadily from 72.8 percent in 1987 to 79.4 percent in 1992 (see Table 5, p.109).

Robberies are violent if they result in great bodily injury, if they involve a firearm, or if they involve the use of another deadly or dangerous weapon in an inhabited dwelling, vessel, or trailer coach. Otherwise, they are "serious only." About 38 percent of robberies involved a firearm in 1992 (Table 6, p. 109). Another 22 percent or so involve other dangerous weapons, and 8 percent of all robberies are residential, so one might expect that roughly 8 percent x 22 percent = 1.8 percent of robberies are of an inhabited dwelling with a deadly or dangerous weapon other than a firearm. We have no data on robberies classified as violent solely because they resulted in great bodily injury.

Assaults (here, restricted to those termed "aggravated assaults" by the FBI) are violent if they result in great bodily injury, involve a firearm, or are committed with intent to commit murder, rape, robbery, or sodomy. Otherwise, they are "serious only." The fraction involving a firearm is 22 percent. Data were not available on the other factors.

Burglary of an inhabited dwelling house, or trailer coach as defined by the Vehicle Code, or inhabited portion of any other building is "serious only." Residential burglaries account for 60 percent of all burglaries (Table 8, p. 110).

No **theft** is deemed violent; only grand theft involving a firearm is considered to be serious.

Arson that causes great bodily injury is defined as violent; all other arson is "serious only." Only 17 percent of arson involves residential property and another 6 percent involves commercial property, so the fraction leading to great bodily injury is likely to be low (see Table 14, p. 116).

C. Tabular Specification of Alternatives

In this appendix, we specify the way that sentencing rules of the various alternatives were input to the model. This is done by means of a set of tables, prefaced by brief discussions, that compare the alternatives on the following dimensions:

- When a felony conviction counts as a "strike"
- Percentage of convictions that result in prison sentences
- Nominal prison sentence
- Reduction in prison sentence for good time.

We conclude with several discrepancies between the inputs to the model and the real-world situation as we now understand it, along with a qualitative assessment of their effects on our results.

Summary Comparison of the Alternative Laws

In general, the effects of the alternatives vary both by the type of crime (minor, serious but not violent, or violent) and by the number of prior strikes. However, patterns sometimes occur across many laws, which makes the comparisons easy. For example, all convictions for a serious felony result in a strike, and only for the Jones three-strikes law and the previous law do convictions for a minor felony result in a strike (see Table C.1). Note that for purposes of our model, *we have made the strike rules for the previous law the same as for the Jones three-strikes law*. We do this because we use the average prison terms served (under the old law) by felons who meet the new strike criteria as a baseline to estimate sentences under the new alternative laws. For example, if an alternative requires a doubling of sentence on the second strike, we assume that average time served is twice the average time served under the previous law for a felon who had a previous serious or violent conviction. (Differences in good-time credits have to be figured in.)

Under the previous law, not all persons convicted of serious felonies went to prison. The rest received jail only or probation sanctions. Under the Jones three-strikes law, all people convicted of a serious felony go to prison if they have at least one prior strike. The guaranteed-full-term alternative would remove this

Table C.1

Does a Felony Conviction Count as a Strike?

Felony Type	Previous Law	Jones 3-Strikes	Jones 2nd-Strike Only	Jones Violent Only	Rainey 3-Strikes	Guaranteed Full Term
			Alternative Law			
If a First Strike						
Minor	No	No	No	No	No	No
Serious	Yes	Yes	Yes	Yes	Yes	Yes
Violent	Yes	Yes	Yes	Yes	Yes	Yes
If a Second Strike						
Minor	No	No	No	No	No	No
Serious	Yes	Yes	Yes	Yes	Yes	Yes
Violent	Yes	Yes	Yes	Yes	Yes	Yes
If a Third Strike						
Minor	Yes	Yes	No	No	No	No
Serious	Yes	Yes	Yes	Yes	Yes	Yes
Violent	Yes	Yes	Yes	Yes	Yes	Yes

NOTE: Regarding previous law, see the text. In this and the following tables, "serious but not violent" is abbreviated to "serious."

last condition, so all serious convictions would result in prison terms; the Jones violent-only law would restrict the 100-percent-prison sanction to violent crimes (see Table C.2).

The nominal prison sentence is the scheduled prison time before subtracting any good time and credit for time served in jail before going to prison. The nominal sentences under the alternative laws are, for the most part, defined in terms of

Table C.2

Percentage of Convictions That Result in Prison Sentences

Felony Type	Previous Law[a]	Jones 3-Strikes	Jones 2nd-Strike Only	Jones Violent Only	Rainey 3-Strikes	Guaranteed Full Term
			Alternative Law			
No Prior Strikes						
Minor	21	21	21	21	21	11
Serious	33	33	33	33	33	100
Violent	30	30	30	30	30	100
One Prior Strike						
Minor	21	21[a]	21[a]	21	21	11
Serious	33	100	100	33	100	100
Violent	30	100	100	100	100	100
Two Prior Strikes						
Minor	21	100	21	21	21	11
Serious	33	100	100	33	100	100
Violent	30	100	100	100	100	100

[a]See the concluding section of this appendix.

the average sentences under the previous law in the crime and strike categories, corrected for good time under that law (i.e., doubled). The exceptions are the 25-year sentences given for third strikes under Jones three-strikes and Rainey and for a violent third strike under Jones violent-only (see Table C.3).

Under the previous law, 50 percent good time was taken off the nominal prison sentence. In other words, actual prison sentences were half what they would have been without the good-time provision. The alternatives to the previous law either keep the good-time sentence cut at 50 percent, or decrease it. For example, the Jones three-strikes law preserves the 50 percent if the conviction is the first strike, but reduces it to 20 percent thereafter. The Rainey three-strikes law goes even further and eliminates good time entirely for violent crimes and for any serious crime on third strike (see Table C.4.)

Discrepancies Between Model Inputs and the Real World

When we began this research, the new three-strikes law had not yet been enacted. Neither the various alternative laws nor legislative experts' understanding of them were firmly settled. Given the complexity of the

Table C.3

Nominal Prison Sentences (Years)[a]

Felony Type	Previous Law	Alternative Law				
		Jones 3-Strikes	Jones 2nd-Strike Only	Jones Violent Only	Rainey 3-Strikes	Guaranteed Full Term
No Prior Strikes						
Minor	2P[b]	N[c]	N	N	N	N
Serious	2P	N	N	N	N	N
Violent	2P	N	N	N	N	N
One Prior Strike						
Minor	2P	2N	2N	N	N	N
Serious	2P	2N	2N	N	N+4.3[d]	N
Violent	2P	2N	2N	2N	N+1.1	N
Two Prior Strikes						
Minor	2P	25	2N	N	N	N
Serious	2P	25	2N	N	25	N
Violent	2P	25	2N	25	25	N

[a]Scheduled prison time before good time and credit for jail time are subtracted.

[b]Data available to us were average sentences *served* under the previous law, designated P. We took the nominal sentence *given* under the previous law to be double that, to account for good time. (P varies by type of crime and number of strikes.)

[c]N = 2P for all cases.

[d]See the concluding section of this appendix.

Table C.4

Percentage Reduction in Prison Sentence for Good Time

Felony Type	Alternative Law					
	Previous Law	Jones 3-Strikes	Jones 2nd-Strike Only	Jones Violent Only	Rainey 3-Strikes	Guaranteed Full Term
No Prior Strikes						
Minor	50	50	50	50	50	50
Serious	50	50	50	50	50	0
Violent	50	50	50	50	0	0
One Prior Strike						
Minor	50	20	20	50	50	50
Serious	50	20	20	50	50	0
Violent	50	20	20	20	0	0
Two Prior Strikes						
Minor	50	20	20	50	50	50
Serious	50	20	20	50	0	0
Violent	50	20	20	20	0	0

NOTE: The difference between 100 percent and the number given above was multiplied by the corresponding entry from Table C.3 to obtain average time served for input to the model. For example, for Jones three-strikes, one prior strike, the input was (100 percent – 20 percent) x 2N = 1.6N = 3.2P.

alternatives and the constraints on data collection inherent in a research project of limited scope, it was inevitable that some model inputs turned out to be erroneous. Here are discrepancies between the model and reality that we have become aware of since the model runs were finished:

- The Jones law requires that those convicted of a minor felony after earning one strike be sent to prison. Our early understanding of the law did not recognize such a requirement, and we did not take account of it in modeling either the new law or the Jones second-strike only alternative. (We did take account of the prison requirement for second-strike serious offenders and for everyone on third strike under the Jones law.) This discrepancy biases our results in the conservative direction. That is, if the model had followed the law on this point, our estimates of both benefits and costs of the Jones law and the second-strike-only alternative would be higher. Because a higher percentage of low-rate offenders' crimes than high-rate offenders' crimes are minor, sanctions aimed at those convicted of minor felonies disproportionately target low-rate offenders and are thus less efficient than those aimed at persons convicted of serious felonies. Therefore, we suspect that we have underestimated benefits less than costs. That is, we have overestimated the cost-effectiveness of the Jones law and the second-strike-only alternative. Because we had already estimated the Jones law to be the most effective, most costly, and least cost-effective alternative, correcting this discrepancy would not change its position relative to other alternatives--with the exception that its effectiveness would actually exceed that of the guaranteed-full-term alternative. However, some adjustment to the provisions of the latter could make up the difference.

- The percentage of convictions resulting in imprisonment under the previous law, given in Table C.2, is based on data from 14 states in U.S. Department of Justice (1992b) (see Table D.6). These numbers do not coincide well with partial California data available from other reliable sources. This discrepancy may arise either from the source of the data in different samples or from lack of sufficient other information available to us about the data to permit proper interpretation. If these numbers are too low, the result would be an overestimate of both the benefit and the cost of the various alternatives. We ran a sensitivity analysis with a different distribution of imprisonment rates (56 percent for violent, 26 percent for serious but not violent, and 20 percent for minor), and found a 9.4 percent decrease in crime reduction and a 5.9 percent decrease in cost (along with a 4.7 percent increase in cost per serious crime prevented). These are well within our stated confidence band of plus or minus 20 percent. However, though the benefit and cost levels eventually achieved are approximately right, the trend graphs we depict in Section 4 probably overestimate the rapidity of the rise in benefits and costs over the next several years. These very early effects stem entirely from differences in imprisonment rates between the Jones law and the previous law.

- We modeled the Rainey three-strikes alternative as if it provided for a sentence enhancement on a second strike for crimes that are serious but not violent. On the basis of the bill's final text, it appears that the only enhancements are for violent offenders (on any strike) and those convicted of any serious offense on third strike. As a result, both the benefit and the cost we cite for the Rainey alternative are somewhat higher than they should be. The difference is unlikely to be enough to change the ranking of that alternative on either dimension.

- The Jones three-strikes law prohibits the accumulation of good-time credits against a prison sentence while an offender is in jail awaiting disposition of his case. The total time incarcerated is thus 80 percent of the nominal prison sentence plus 20 percent of the jail time served. We interpreted the law to prohibit *any* allowance for jail time served in deciding an offender's release date from prison. That is, we assumed a total time incarcerated equal to 80 percent of the nominal prison sentence plus all the jail time served. Correcting the discrepancy—subtracting 80 percent of the jail time served— would translate into incarceration times only a few months shorter and would have only a very small effect on the results.

D. Parameter Estimates

It is difficult to estimate the numbers of offenses low- and high-rate offenders commit per year. The offense rates are even difficult to define, because they depend upon which crimes are included in the offense count ("serious" and "violent" crimes as defined by California law are a subset of the FBI's index crimes, which in turn are a subset of all felonies). Moreover, the rates depend upon the portions of offenders classified as low and high rate. Here we *define* low- and high-rate offenders by halving California's 1993 incarcerated population. The half with the lower offense rates is defined to be low-rate offenders, and the half with the higher offense rates is defined to be high-rate offenders.

In addition to the offense rates for each group of offenders and each type of crime, the model also requires information about the following variables: the number of low- and high-rate offenders on the street, probabilities that various offenses will lead to an arrest, the rate at which offenders are arrested for nonindex crimes, and the proportion of active criminals who desist, or stop being criminals, each year.

The offense rates and other parameters can be estimated by insisting that the behavior of the model implied by these parameters agree with the observed behavior of criminals and of the criminal justice system. In particular, the model's results must match what is known about the numbers of active felons, offenses, arrests, and people incarcerated, as well as the rate at which people released from prison are rearrested (recidivism).

The plan of this appendix is to give the results, the parameter estimates, first. Then it gives the facts upon which the estimates are based. Finally, it gives the system of equations that link the unknown parameters to the known facts, and whose solution provides the estimates of the parameters.

Results

The estimated parameters are given in Tables D.1 through D.4, surrounded by a few facts (such as the numbers of offenses and the numbers of arrests) that provide context for the estimates. The key parameters on which to focus are the

Table D.1

Offense Rates by FBI Index Categories Allocated to California Law Categories

California	FBI Index Crimes								
Categories	Murder	Rape	Robbery	Assault	Burglary	Theft	MVT	Arson	Total
Low-Rate Offenders									
Violent	0.0011	0.0138	0.0324	0.0687	0.0000	0.0000	0.0000	0.0002	0.1161
Serious	0.0000	0.0034	0.0485	0.0687	0.1616	0.0000	0.0000	0.0047	0.2869
Minor	0.0000	0.0000	0.0000	0.0000	0.1077	0.3688	0.2328	0.0000	0.7093
Total	0.0011	0.0172	0.0809	0.1373	0.2693	0.3688	0.2328	0.0049	1.1124
High-Rate Offenders									
Violent	0.0187	0.2412	0.5669	1.2032	0.0000	0.0000	0.0000	0.0043	2.0343
Serious	0.0000	0.0603	0.8504	1.2032	2.8306	0.0000	0.0000	0.0823	5.0268
Minor	0.0000	0.0000	0.0000	0.0000	1.8871	6.4620	4.0786	0.0000	12.4277
Total	0.0187	0.3016	1.4173	2.4063	4.7177	6.4620	4.0786	0.0867	19.4889
Average Offender									
Violent	0.0045	0.0585	0.1376	0.2920	0.0000	0.0000	0.0000	0.0011	0.4937
Serious	0.0000	0.0146	0.2064	0.2920	0.6869	0.0000	0.0000	0.0200	1.2199
Minor	0.0000	0.0000	0.0000	0.0000	0.4579	1.5682	0.9898	0.0000	3.0159
Total	0.0045	0.0732	0.3439	0.5840	1.1449	1.5682	0.9898	0.0210	4.7295

NOTES: Only the thefts in the FBI index that are felonies in California (about a third) are counted in our analyses. Offense rate = offenses per offender per year.

Table D.2

Offense Rates by Index Crime

	FBI Index Crimes								
Item	Murder	Rape	Robbery	Assault	Burglary	Theft	MVT	Arson	Total
Adult offenses	4493	72579	341109	579144	1135441	1555253	981628	20861	4690507
Low offense rate	0.0011	0.0172	0.0809	0.1373	0.2693	0.3688	0.2328	0.0049	1.1124
High offense rate	0.0187	0.3016	1.4173	2.4063	4.7177	6.4620	4.0786	0.0867	19.4889
Average offense rate	0.0045	0.0732	0.3439	0.5840	1.1449	1.5682	0.9898	0.0210	4.7295

NOTES: Only the thefts in the FBI index that are felonies in California (about a third) are counted in our analyses. Offense rate = offenses per offender per year.

low- and high-rate offense rates in Tables D.1 and D.2, and the number of low- and high-rate offenders on the street (Table D.4)

Basis in California Criminal Justice Data

As mentioned above, the parameter estimates given in Tables D.1 through D.4 are derived from equations that take as input current California data for arrests, convictions, and sentences. Those data are shown in Tables D.5 through D.7.

Table D.3

Arrest Rates by Index Crime

Item	FBI Index Crimes								
	Murder	Rape	Robbery	Assault	Burglary	Theft	MVT	Arson	Total
Adult arrests	2970	3471	22990	97695	55286	50994	28221	1048	262675
Low arrest rate	1.112	0.080	0.113	0.284	0.082	0.055	0.048	0.085	1.860
High arrest rate	0.556	0.040	0.057	0.142	0.041	0.028	0.024	0.042	0.930
Average arrest rate	0.661	0.048	0.067	0.169	0.049	0.033	0.029	0.050	1.105

NOTES: Arrest rate = arrests per offense. Low arrest rate = arrest rate for low-rate offender. High arrest rate = arrest rate for high-rate offender. The estimate that arrest rates for high-rate offenders are half those for low-rate offenders comes from Greenwood and Turner, 1987, pp. 33 and 48.

Table D.4

Estimates of Other Parameters

Parameter	Estimate
Ratio of high- to low-rate offense rates	17.52
Number of active offenders on street	
Low-rate offenders	796,550
High-rate offenders	195,211
Arrests per year for nonindex crimes:	
Low-rate offenders	0.2167
High-rate offenders	0.1842
Annual desistance rate	
Low-rate offenders	0.100
High-rate offenders	0.050

In addition to the data in Tables D.5 through D.7, the parameter estimation in this appendix requires information on the pace at which people who are released from prison get rearrested, and on the total number of criminals on the street in California. We obtained the arrest recidivism rates from Beck (1989, p. 3), where the percentage of people released from prison who have been rearrested within one year is 39.3, within two years is 54.5, and within three years is 62.5.

We estimated the number of criminals on the street using the 1991 National Household Survey on Drug Abuse (NHSDA). In that survey, 2.57 percent of adults responded that they had committed a felony during the previous year. Specifically, those respondents said that in the last 12 months they had taken a car not belonging to them, used force to get money from a person, broken into a house, hurt someone badly enough to need a doctor, used a weapon to get something from a person, sold an illegal drug, or had been arrested in the last 12 months for one of the following crimes: larceny, theft, burglary, aggravated assault, motor vehicle theft, robbery, rape, murder, other offenses against

Table D.5

Felonies and Felony Arrests: California, 1992

Item	Violent Crimes[a]				Property Crimes[a]				Other Crimes		Total
	Murder[b]	Rape	Robbery	Assault	Burglary	Theft	MVT	Arson	Drug	Other[c]	
Reported crimes	4158	12790	131154	200754	428852	370418	594183	21979			1764288
Reporting rate	1.000	0.167	0.545	0.469	0.499	0.380	0.737	1.000			
Total crimes	4158	76740	240650	428047	859423	974784	806218	21979			3411999
Offenders per crime	1.32	1.10	1.92	1.52	1.92	1.92	1.92	1.92			
Juvenile crimes	754	10759	62989	47031	268048	164757	294954	11114			860405
Juvenile offenses	995	11835	120939	71487	514651	316333	566312	21339			1623890
Juvenile arrests	658	566	8151	12059	25059	10372	16281	1072	7636	11697	93551
Juvenile arrest rate (%)[d]	66.10	4.78	6.74	16.87	4.87	3.28	2.87	5.02			
Adult crimes	3404	65981	177661	381016	591375	810027	511264	10865			2551594
Adult offenses	4493	72579	341109	579144	1135441	1555253	981628	20861			4690507
Adult arrests	2970	3471	22990	97695	55286	50994	28221	1048	127812	80713	471200
Adult arrest rate (%)[d]	66.10	4.78	6.74	16.87	4.87	3.28	2.87	5.02			

SOURCES: Data on index crimes and arrests, except arson, are from FBI (1993), Table 5. The data were adjusted by the authors using the California Department of Justice *1992 Arrest and Citation Register* (1992b) (theft is the major change; only 38 percent of FBI index thefts are felonies in California). Data on nonindex crimes and arrests, plus arson, are from California Department of Justice (1992a). Data on the reporting rate are from U.S. Department of Justice (1992a). Rape reporting rate is from National Victim Center (1992), p. 5.

[a]"Violent" crime and "property" crime, as defined here, sum to FBI "index" crimes.

[b]Total crimes prorated to juveniles and adults in proportion to juvenile and adult arrests within each type of crime.

[c]Other category includes the "kidnapping," "forgery," and "all other" categories in the state report.

[d]"Arrest rate" is arrests per 100 offenses.

Table D.6

Adult Convictions and Sanctions for Felonies: California, 1992

Item	Violent Crimes				Property Crimes				Other Crimes		Total
	Murder	Rape	Robbery	Assault	Burglary	Theft	MVT	Arson	Drug	Other	
Arrests	2970	3471	22990	97695	55286	50994	28221	1048	127812	80713	471200
Convictions / arrest	0.6800	0.4800	0.5300	0.4600	0.7000	0.6500	0.4700	0.6100	0.5800	0.6500	0.5797
Convictions	2020	1666	12185	44940	38700	33146	13264	639	74131	52463	273154
No incarceration	162	133	1584	14830	5805	10275	2918	160	13344	16264	65474
Jail only	222	283	2924	23369	17415	17899	8091	268	42255	28330	141057
Prison	1636	1250	7676	6741	15480	4972	2255	211	18533	7870	66623
Rates (per conviction)											
No incarceration	0.0800	0.0800	0.1300	0.3300	0.1500	0.3100	0.2200	0.2500	0.1800	0.3100	0.2397
Jail only	0.1100	0.1700	0.2400	0.5200	0.4500	0.5400	0.6100	0.4200	0.5700	0.5400	0.5164
Prison	0.8100	0.7500	0.6300	0.1500	0.4000	0.1500	0.1700	0.3300	0.2500	0.1500	0.2439

SOURCES: U.S. Department of Justice (1992b), conviction rates from Table 5.53, p. 546; disposition from Table 5.57, p. 549. The conviction rates are from eight states, and the disposition rates are from 14 states. Both groups include California. Rates per conviction for "other" are assumed to be the same as those for "theft."

Table D.7

Actual Time Served in Jail and Prison Sanctions: California, 1990

Item	Violent Crimes				Property Crimes				Other Crimes		Total
	Murder	Rape	Robbery	Assault	Burglary	Theft	MVT	Arson	Drug	Other	
Jail-only sentences	222	283	2924	23369	17415	17899	8091	268	42255	28330	141057
Prison sentences	1636	1250	7676	6741	15480	4972	2255	211	18533	7870	66623
Jail sanction											
Average time (mo)	4	4	4	4	4	4	4	4	4	4	4
Total person-yr[a]	74	94	975	7790	5805	5966	2697	89	14085	9443	47019
Prison sanction											
Average jail time (mo)[b]	7.0	6.7	5.1	5.7	4.5	3.9	4.1	6.4	4.7	3.5	4.7
Average prison time (mo)	43.5	51.5	30.4	25.4	20.0	12.4	12.1	19.8	14.6	12.0	19.6
Average incarceration (mo)	50.5	58.2	35.5	31.1	24.5	16.3	16.2	26.2	19.3	15.5	24.3
Total jail person-yr	954	698	3262	3202	5805	1616	770	113	7259	2295	25974
Total prison person-yr	5926	5365	19421	14277	25813	5146	2269	348	22556	7843	108964
Total combined person-yr	6880	6062	22684	17479	31618	6762	3039	460	29815	10139	134938

SOURCES: California Department of Corrections (1991) is the source for the prison sentences and the jail sentences before prison. However, the 4-month jail-only sentences are hypothetical.

a"Person-years" served in jail or prison equals the count of sentences times the jail or prison time in years. This would equal the jail and prison populations in steady state.

bAverage time to first parole, times 1.15, which accounts for average time served for parole revocation. Parole violators return to do an estimated 15 percent additional time on average. This estimate is calculated as follows: 74 percent of parolees return and get an average of 6.9 months additional sentence, of which half is served; and (0.74)(6.9/2)/16.5 = 0.15.

persons, or arson. Not all possible felony offenses are listed, but, on the other hand, some of the actions listed might not constitute crimes (e.g., hurting someone badly in self-defense).

Applying the 2.57 percent to the 22,680,000 adults in California in 1992 yields an estimate of 583,566 adult felons in California. However, this estimate must be corrected for underreporting and populations missed by the household survey. We estimated the undercount to be 41.2 percent by comparing the number of people reporting arrests with known numbers of arrests for crime categories with large numbers of crimes (see Table D.8). The corrected estimate is 991,761 adult felons on the street in California in 1992.

The NHSDA is a very large, anonymous, and well-run survey, but its principal focus is drug use, not other crime, so we wanted to confirm in some way that it is reliable for this purpose. Obtaining such confirmation is very difficult, but we could compare responses of the National Youth Survey (NYS), which is generally regarded as a reasonably good survey for criminal behavior for youth, and the NHSDA.

The most recent year for which NYS data were available was 1980. We compared the average prevalences of various criminal acts for the 15–21-year-old NYS respondents to those of similarly aged respondents in the 1991 NHSDA. The definitions of criminal acts were not always comparable (particularly for theft; see Table D.9). Nevertheless, the fractions of respondents reporting the various activities (see Table D.10) did not reveal any systematic tendency for the NHSDA respondents to be either more or less forthcoming than those of the NYS, lending some circumstantial reassurance to the reasonableness of using the NHSDA to estimate the number of offenders.

Table D.8

Using Arrests to Estimate Underreporting of Crime Commission

Item	Robbery	Assault	Burglary	Theft	MVT	All
Observed adult arrests	22950	96594	55124	114990	28414	318072
NHSDA/observed arrests	0.400	0.388	0.679	0.529	0.442	
Fraction of arrests incarcerated	0.334	0.070	0.280	0.098	0.080	
Underreporting fraction	0.399	0.583	0.057	0.414	0.520	
Arrests times underreporting	9166	56295	3139	47551	14763	130914
Wgt. average underreporting						0.412

NOTE: NHSDA estimate = (observed arrests) (1 - fraction incarcerated) (reporting fraction).

Table D.9

NYS Variables Compared to NHSDA Variables

NYS Variable	NHSDA Variable	NHSDA Description
Felony assault	hurtbad	Hurt someone enough to need a doctor
Minor assault	phyfight	Gotten into a physical fight
Robbery	forcemon or	Used force to get money from a person
	gunmoney	Used weapon to get something from a person
Felony theft	strsteal	Taken something from a store without paying
Minor theft	othsteal	Taken something not belonging to you
Damaged property	damage	Damaged property not belonging to you
Crimes against persons	forcemon or gunmoney or hurtbad or phyfight	See above
General theft	strsteal or othsteal	See above

NOTE: NHSDA descriptions include actions that are not necessarily crimes.

Table D.10

Percentage of Respondents Reporting Criminal Activity: NYS Compared to NHSDA

Offense	NYS	NHSDA
Felony assault	8.6	6.9
Minor assault	19.9	24.3
Robbery	1.9	1.3
Felony theft	8.4	11.6
Minor theft	14.4	9.6
Damaged property	15.1	9.8
Crimes against persons	23.3	24.8
General theft	18.0	16.7

Equations Defining Offense Rates and Related Parameters

The parameters are estimated by solving equations implied by the facts about California's criminal justice system described above. Equation (1) below simply requires that the sum of the number of low- and high-rate offenders equal the total number of active felons. Equations (2) through (9) require that the modeled number of offenses equal the actual number. Similarly, Equations (10) through (18) equate the modeled and observed numbers of arrests. Equation (19) ensures that high-rate offenders do indeed make up half the prison population, and Equations (20) through (22) match the modeled and observed recidivism rates.

These 22 equations can be solved for the 22 unknown parameters, yielding the results summarized in Section 4.

Unknown Parameters

There are 22 unknowns:

2 counts of offenders on street, low rate and high rate, L and H

8 offense rates, offenses per offender per year, for low-rate offenders doing eight types of index crimes, λ_i.

1 multiplier to convert low-rate lambdas into high-rate lambdas, m (same multiplier for all index crimes).

8 arrest rates (probability that an offense will result in an arrest) for low-rate offenders doing eight types of index crimes, α_i; the arrest rate for high-rate offenders is estimated to be 0.5 times that for low-rate offenders, where the 0.5 estimate comes from Greenwood and Turner (1987, pp. 33 and 48).

1 annual number of arrests per low-rate offender for nonindex crimes, w; the annual number of arrests per high-rate offender for nonindex crimes is estimated to be 0.85 times that for low-rate offenders, where the 0.85 was estimated from information in the RAND Inmate Survey (Chaiken and Chaiken, 1982).

2 annual desistance rates, d_l and d_h, the proportions of low- and high-rate active (or potentially active incarcerated) criminals who stop being criminals each year.

Street Population Equation

The number of active felons on the street is 991,761, estimated from the NHSDA.

$$L + H = 991,761 \qquad (1)$$

L = low-rate offenders on the street

H = high-rate offenders on the street

Offense Equations

Offenders times offense rate equals offenses (index crimes).

$$L\lambda_i + Hm\lambda_i = \text{type } i \text{ index offenses per year;} \quad i = 1 \text{ to } 8 \qquad (2\text{–}9)$$

62

λ_i = type i index offenses per low-rate offender per year

m = ratio of high-rate offense rate to low-rate offense rate

Arrest Equations

Offenses times arrest rate equals arrests (index crimes).

$$L\lambda_i\alpha_i + Hm\lambda_i 0.5\alpha_i = \text{arrests for type } i \text{ index offense; } \quad i = 1 \text{ to } 8 \quad (10\text{--}17)$$

α_i = arrest rate for low-rate offenders (arrests per offense)

Offenders times arrests per offender equals arrests for nonindex crimes.

$$Lw + 0.85Hw = \text{nonindex offense arrests per year} \quad (18)$$

w = arrests per nonindex offense per offender, for low-rate offenders

Incarcerated Population Equation

Low-rate offenders equal high-rate offenders in the incarcerated population of felons.

$$\sum_{i=1}^{8}\left[L\lambda_i\alpha_i c_i\left(j_i s_{ji} + p_i s_{pi}\right)\right] + Lwc_n\left(j_n s_{jn} + p_n s_{pn}\right)$$
$$= \sum_{i=1}^{8}\left[Hm\lambda_i 0.5\alpha_i c_i\left(j_i s_{ji} + p_i s_{pi}\right)\right] + 0.85Hwc_n\left(j_n s_{jn} + p_n s_{pn}\right) \quad (19)$$

c_i = conviction rate for index crime i (convictions per arrest)

c_n = conviction rate for nonindex crimes

j_i = jail-only rate for index crime i (jail sanctions per arrest)

j_n = jail-only rate for nonindex crime

p_i = imprisonment rate for index crime i (prison sanctions per arrest)

p_n = imprisonment rates for nonindex crimes

s_{ji} = jail-only sentence for index crime i

s_{pi} = prison-sanction sentence (including jail time) for index crime

s_{jn} = jail-only sentence for nonindex crime i

s_{pn} = prison-sanction sentence (including jail time) for nonindex crime

Recidivism Equations

39.3 percent of those released from prison are rearrested at least once during their first year out of prison, 54.5 percent in two years, and 62.5 percent in three years.

$$\frac{X_{nl} + X_{nh}}{E_l + E_h} = 0.393 \text{ if } n = 1,\ 0.545 \text{ if } n = 2,\ 0.625 \text{ if } n = 3 \qquad (20\text{–}22)$$

E_l = low-rate offenders exiting from prison annually

E_h = high-rate offenders exiting from prison annually

F_l = low-rate offenders still active when they exit prison

F_h = high-rate offenders still active when they exit prison

A_l = arrests of low-rate offenders during first year out of prison (including multiple arrests)

A_h = arrests of high-rate offenders during first year out of prison (including multiple arrests)

X_{nl} = low-rate offenders exiting from prison who are arrested at least once during n years out of prison

X_{nh} = high-rate offenders exiting from prison who are arrested at least once during n years out of prison

$$E_l = \sum_{i=1}^{8}\left[L\lambda_i \alpha_i c_i p_i\right] + Lwc_n p_n$$

$$E_h = \sum_{i=1}^{8}\left[Hm\lambda_i 0.5\alpha_i c_i p_i\right] + H0.85wc_n p_n$$

$$F_l = \sum_{i=1}^{8}\left[L\lambda_i \alpha_i c_i p_i (1 - d_l)^{s_{pi}}\right] + Lwc_n p_n (1 - d_l)^{s_{pn}}$$

$$F_h = \sum_{i=1}^{8}\left[Hm\lambda_i 0.5\alpha_i c_i p_i (1 - d_h)^{s_{pi}}\right] + H0.85wc_n p_n (1 - d_h)^{s_{pn}}$$

d_l = desistance rate for low-rate offenders during prison sanction (fraction of active criminals, ones that would be active if not incarcerated, who become inactive per year)

d_h = desistance rate for high-rate offenders during prison sanction

$$A_l = F_l \left[\sum_{i=1}^{8} \left(\lambda_i \alpha_i \right) + w \right]$$

$$A_h = F_h \left[\sum_{i=1}^{8} \left(m\lambda_i 0.5\alpha_i \right) + 0.85w \right]$$

$$X_{nl} = F_l \left[\frac{r_l}{r_l + d_l} \right] \left[1 - e^{-n(r_l + d_l)} \right]$$

$$X_{nh} = F_h \left[\frac{r_h}{r_h + d_h} \right] \left[1 - e^{-n(r_h + d_h)} \right]$$

$r_l = A_l / F_l$ = arrest rate of low-rate offenders exiting from prison

$r_h = A_h / F_h$ = arrest rate of high-rate offenders exiting from prison

E. Model Implementation

The three-strikes model is programmed in Excel 4, and consists of five components each of which is on its own spreadsheet (see Figure E.1). MACROS contains the instructions that automate model operation. INOUT contains the inputs that define each policy option, primarily the felony disposition information presented in Appendix C, but also behavioral parameters some of which are sometimes influenced by policy (see below). INOUT also is the place where results are stored so the inputs defining a policy and the consequences of that policy can be reported together. The results of an analysis run with the three-strikes model are summarized in Section 4.

The main work of the model is done in the ANNUAL component. There the street and incarcerated populations at the start of a given year are projected to the end of that year, taking account of flow into and out of active (or potentially active) criminal status, and flows into and out of incarceration. The results of each successive annual projection are stored temporarily in PROJYRS (temporary in the sense that when a new policy is analyzed the results in PROJYRS from an earlier analysis are displaced). After completing 25 projection years, final outputs (costs, crimes, and population counts) are computed in the PROJYRS component. These results for the plan being analyzed are then copied to the INOUT component for more permanent storage.

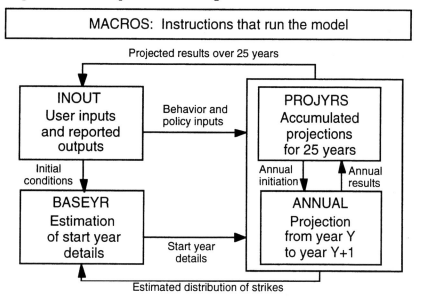

Figure E.1—Components of the Three-Strikes Model

The BASEYR component contains the initial conditions (those for 1993) from which projections start. These initial conditions vary by policy because a key element is the distribution of street and incarcerated populations across numbers of strikes. The definition of strikes varies by policy, so the distribution by strikes also varies. Ideally, these initial conditions would be known from surveys of street populations and administrative records, supplemented by surveys, for incarcerated populations. Unfortunately, records and surveys that would completely define initial conditions do not exist (although, given enough resources, useful partial information could be gleaned from the surveys and records that do exist). For this analysis, we adopted the approach of running the model for data from previous years under different policies to arrive at distributions by strikes under those policies. However, time and resources did not permit a rigorous modeling of the dynamics of past behavior. Rather, all we did is find the steady state implied by current conditions. We judge that this approach to determining initial conditions, although less than ideal (modeling past dynamics properly would be preferable), is adequate for this analysis.

The behavioral parameter inputs to the three-strikes model are given in Tables E.1 and E.2, for the previous and the three-strikes laws, respectively. Only the trial rate inputs differ between these two laws, with trial rates assumed to be higher under the three-strikes law because of the threat of greater sanctions.

Note that the desistance rate for high-rate offenders in the model inputs is 0.075, and not the 0.050 estimated in Appendix D. The reason is that data from other research (Blumstein et al., 1986) suggests that a ten-year criminal career for high-rate offenders is about right (implying a 0.100 desistance rate). For the analysis in this report, we averaged the two estimates to get the 0.075.

Note also that the split between high- and low-rate incarcerated offenders is 60 percent high-rate and 40 percent low-rate in these model inputs, rather than the 50-50 split adopted by definition in Appendix D. The 60-40 split resulted when the model was used to estimate initial conditions (as of the end of 1993) by running it to its steady state using a constant incidence scenario.

We have discussed the model's shortcomings elsewhere (see Section 3, for example). To these, we add that the annual time step chosen for this model is not ideal; a quarter-year time step would be better. For example, the average sentences by number of strikes for minor crimes under the previous law are estimated by this analysis to be 1, 2, and 3 years. It may well be that 1.25, 1.75, 3.00 is a more accurate representation of actual average sentences by number of strikes, but in the current model there is no way to test that hypothesis.

Table E.1

Behavioral Parameter Inputs to Analysis of Previous Law

Offenders on Street, and Arrests per Offender per Year

Type of Offender	Offenders, Start 1993		Arrests per Offender per Year			Convictions per Arrest		
	On Street	In Jail or Prison	Violent	Serious	Minor	Violent	Serious	Minor
Low-rate	778741	73287	0.025	0.039	0.257	0.481	0.553	0.608
High-rate	203309	107647	0.223	0.341	0.538	0.481	0.553	0.608

NOTE: "Serious" excludes violent.

Desistance and Deterrence

Type of Offender	Desistance Rate[a]		Deterrence Probability[b]
	On Street	Incarcerated	
Low-rate	0.100	0.100	0.00
High-rate	0.075	0.075	0.00

[a]Probability of desisting in a given year.
[b]Probability of deterrence by threat of third-strike penalty (i.e., one-shot desistance in the year offender gets second strike, in addition to street desistance for that year).

Trials per Arrest

Type of Offense	Prior Strikes		
	0	1	2+
Minor	0.025	0.030	0.035
Serious	0.030	0.035	0.040
Violent	0.035	0.040	0.045

NOTE: "Serious" excludes violent.

Annual Number of New Offenders (under reference desistance assumptions)

Projection Year	Calendar Year	Low-Rate Offenders	High-Rate Offenders
Base	1993	84917	20838
1	1994	91353	22944
2	1995	94930	24009
3	1996	100765	25811
4	1997	102333	26216
5	1998	103845	26600
6	1999	105454	27015
7	2000	107034	27418
8	2001	109470	28100
9	2002	111253	28560
10	2003	113008	29008
11	2004	114839	29480
12	2005	116670	29949
13	2006	118525	30424
14	2007	120432	30914
15	2008	122392	31420
16	2009	124329	31915
17	2010	126316	32425
18	2011	128358	32950
19	2012	130403	33474
20	2013	132501	34013
21	2014	134630	34560
22	2015	136761	35105
23	2016	138973	35674
24	2017	141218	36252
25	2018	143468	36828

Table E.2

Behavioral Parameter Inputs to Analysis of Three-Strikes Law

Offenders on Street, and Arrests per Offender per Year

Type of Offender	Offenders, Start 1993		Arrests per Offender per Year			Convictions per Arrest		
	On Street	In Jail or Prison	Violent	Serious	Minor	Violent	Serious	Minor
Low-rate	778741	73287	0.025	0.039	0.257	0.481	0.553	0.608
High-rate	203309	107647	0.223	0.341	0.538	0.481	0.553	0.608

NOTE: "Serious" excludes violent.

Desistance and Deterrence

Type of Offender	Desistance Rate[a]		Deterrence Probability[b]
	Street	Incarcerated	
Low-rate	0.100	0.100	0.00
High-rate	0.075	0.075	0.00

[a]Probability of desisting in a given year.
[b]Probability of deterrence by threat of third-strike penalty (i.e., one-shot desistance in the year offender gets second strike, in addition to street desistance for that year).

Trials per Arrest

Type of Offense	Prior Strikes		
	0	1	2+
Minor	0.025	0.030	0.070
Serious	0.030	0.070	0.080
Violent	0.035	0.080	0.090

NOTE: "Serious" excludes violent.

Annual Number of New Offenders (under reference desistance assumptions)

Projection Year	Calendar Year	Low-Rate Offenders	High-Rate Offenders
Base	1993	84917	20838
1	1994	91353	22944
2	1995	94930	24009
3	1996	100765	25811
4	1997	102333	26216
5	1998	103845	26600
6	1999	105454	27015
7	2000	107034	27418
8	2001	109470	28100
9	2002	111253	28560
10	2003	113008	29008
11	2004	114839	29480
12	2005	116670	29949
13	2006	118525	30424
14	2007	120432	30914
15	2008	122392	31420
16	2009	124329	31915
17	2010	126316	32425
18	2011	128358	32950
19	2012	130403	33474
20	2013	132501	34013
21	2014	134630	34560
22	2015	136761	35105
23	2016	138973	35674
24	2017	141218	36252
25	2018	143468	36828

References

Beck, Allen J. (1989), *Recidivism of Prisoners Released in 1983*, U.S. Department of Justice, Bureau of Justice Statistics Special Report, Washington, D.C., April.

Blumstein, A., J. Cohen, and D. Nagin (1978), *Deterrence and Incapacitation: Estimating the Effects of Criminal Sanctions on Crime Rates*, National Academy of Sciences, Washington, D.C.

Blumstein, Alfred, et al., eds. (1986), *Criminal Careers and "Career Criminals,"* Vol. I, National Research Council, National Academy of Sciences, Washington, D.C.

California Department of Corrections (1991), *California Prisoners and Parolees, 1990*, Youth and Adult Correctional Agency, Sacramento, California.

California Department of Justice (1992a), *Crime and Delinquency in California, 1992*, Division of Law Enforcement, Law Enforcement Information Center, Sacramento, California.

California Department of Justice (1992b), *1992 Arrest and Citation Register*, Sacramento, California.

Chaiken, Jan M., and Marcia R. Chaiken (1982), *Varieties of Criminal Behavior*, RAND, R-2814-NIJ, August.

Cook, P. (1980), "Research in Criminal Deterrence: Laying the Groundwork for the Second Decade," in N. Morris and M. Tonry, eds., *Crime and Justice: An Annual Review of Research*, Vol. 2, the University of Chicago Press, Chicago, Illinois.

Federal Bureau of Investigation (1993), *Uniform Crime Reports for the United States—1992*, U.S. Department of Justice, Washington, D.C., October.

Greenwood, Peter W., and Susan Turner (1987), *Selective Incapacitation Revisited: Why the High-Rate Offenders Are Hard To Predict*, RAND, R-3397-NIJ, March.

Keeler, Emmett B., and Shan Cretin (1983), "Discounting of Life-Saving and Other Nonmonetary Effects," *Management Science*, Vol. 29, No. 3, pp. 300–306.

MacCoun, D. (1993), "Drugs and the Law: A Psychological Analysis of Drug Prohibition," *Psychological Bulletin*, Vol. 111, No. 3, pp. 497–512.

National Victim Center (1992), *Rape in America: A Report to the Nation*, Crime Victims Research and Treatment Center, Charleston, South Carolina, April.

Rohter, Larry (1994), "States Embracing Tougher Measures for Fighting Crime: *The New York Times*, May 10, p. 1.

Shinnar, Shlomo, and Revel Shinnar (1975), "The Effects of the Criminal Justice System on the Control of Crime: A Quantitative Approach," *Law and Society Review*, Vol. 9, No. 4, pp. 581–611.

U.S. Department of Justice (1992a), *Crime Victimization in the United States, 1991*, A National Crime Victimization Survey Report, NCJ-139563, Office of Justice Programs, Bureau of Justice Statistics, December.

U.S. Department of Justice (1992b), *Source Book of Criminal Justice Statistics—1991*, Bureau of Justice Statistics, Washington, D.C.